C. L. R. James

This photograph taken in the United States in 1940 shows C. L. R. James as the author knew him. He was a little better dressed than he was in London in the thirties, and he looks a little more arrogant than he did then. The photograph was given to the author by Blackwell Books, having appeared in one of their books about James.

C. L. R. James

MEMORIES
and Commentaries

Louise Cripps

Cornwall Books
New York • London

© 1997 by Rosemont Publishing and Printing Corporation

All rights reserved. Authorization to photocopy items for internal or personal use, or the internal or personal use of specific clients, is granted by the copyright owner, provided that a base fee of $10.00, plus eight cents per page, per copy is paid directly to the Copyright Clearance Center, 222 Rosewood Drive, Danvers, Massachusetts 01923. [0-8453-4865-5/97 $10.00 + 8¢ pp, pc.]

Cornwall Books
440 Forsgate Drive
Cranbury, NJ 08512

Cornwall Books
16 Barter Street
London WC1A 2AH, England

Cornwall Books
P.O. Box 338, Port Credit
Mississauga, Ontario
Canada L5G 4L8

The paper used in this publication meets the requirements of the American National Standard for Permanence of Paper for Printed Library Materials Z39.48–1984.

Library of Congress Cataloging-in-Publication Data

Samoiloff, Louise Cripps.
    C.L.R. James : memories and commentaries / Louise Cripps Samoiloff
      p. cm.
    ISBN 0-8453-4865-5 (alk. paper)
    1. James, C. L. R. (Cyril Lionel Robert), 1901– . 2. Authors, Trinidadian—20th century—Biography. 3. Revolutionaries—Trinidad—Biography. 4. Historians—Trinidad—Biography. 5. Politics and literature—History—20th century. 6. Communism—History—20th century. 7. Samoiloff, Louise Cripps. I. Title.
PR9272.9.J35Z87   1997
818—dc20
[B]
                                                                   96-43630
                                                                      CIP

PRINTED IN THE UNITED STATES OF AMERICA

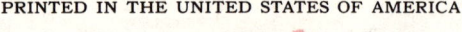

Contents

Part One: Memories

1. First Meeting — 11
2. The Marxist Group — 22
3. Background of World Events — 37
4. James and I Go to Paris — 48
5. Love Affair — 55
6. Consequences — 70
7. New York — 81

Part Two: Separate Ways

8. Separate Ways: CLR — 97
9. Separate Ways: LLC — 108
10. Contacts and Correspondence — 117

Part Three: Looking Back

11. Looking Back — 133
12. James and Women — 145

Part Four: Commentary

13. James's Books — 159
14. James's Political Paths — 176
15. James and His Late Admirers — 187

Part One
Memories

1

First Meeting

I FIRST MET C. L. R. JAMES AT THE HOME OF DR. ISRAEL HIEGER and his wife, Esther, in Hampstead Garden Suburb, London. There were eight of us to dinner. I noticed the West Indian sitting at the other end of the table. My husband and I had arrived late, even though we only lived around the corner. I had a terrible headache, and while I was aware that James was more or less monopolizing the conversation at the dinner table with everyone listening, I was concentrating on my headache. Luckily I had a doctor as my dinner partner.

I was playing with the food, and he asked me what was the matter. I told him I had this splitting headache. He said: "Now eat up all your food; fill your stomach as much as possible." He then put his hand into his waistcoat pocket and produced a small packet of aspirins. He said: "Now eat up and when you've finished, have some water and take three aspirins. I will absolutely guarantee that the headache will go." So I concentrated on eating the food and then took the aspirins. He was right; the headache disappeared.

After dinner had finished, we went to sit in a horseshoe circle at the fireplace. I am not sure what the weather was, but I have a feeling that it was autumn but there was no fire burning. I believe it was the autumn of 1933.

By this time I could concentrate on James. He was very tall, lean, handsome; I started to find him as fascinating as the others had done. He was telling us about Trotsky and the perfidies of Stalin; also, how the Communists in Great Britain were telling lots of lies and pursuing wrong policies. Normally, no one person monopolizes the conversation, and if they try, the others around feel somewhat irritated. In this case, however, everybody was completely fascinated by James. They would ask questions; I do not know if I did or not, but everyone was quite prepared and pleased to have him, more or less, give us a lecture on his subjects. He had been a teacher in Trinidad and liked the role.

V. S. Naipual, James's countryman, writing of the character Lebrun in his novel *A Way in the World* (1994), describes a dinner party in Maida Vale, London, when CLR (Lebrun) was then more than fifty. I was reminded strongly of the dinner party at which I had first met him. All the visitors there had been asked just to hear James talk. Naipual's portrait is one that I recognized, most of all when he calls James "a born talker." Naipual writes: "He was slender and fine-featured. Close to, he was delicate, smooth-skinned with a touch of copper in his dark complexion. . . . It was understood we had come to hear him talk. Soon enough Lebrun (James) was launched. He was born to talk."

I have not read any other book about James that brought him so vividly to mind. The description of him at that small dinner party, thirty years later, was so close to the one when I had first met him, all of us listening to him intensely. All the people in the room at that earlier dinner party had been brought there just to hear James talk. I was the exception and had not fully understood that was why the dinner party had been arranged.

During the coming weeks, Esther Hieger came to see me and asked me if I would like to join her in going to James's place where there was going to be a meeting of sympathetic people to form what I understood was a Trotskyist group.

At that time, I had just lost a full-term baby with a placenta previa; the child had suffocated, and I had almost died and needed two blood transfusions, so that I was no longer working, as I had been until late in my pregnancy. I was in a relatively sad and unhappy mood, and this possibility of going and hearing James again offered a much needed diversion. I had been enchanted by him that first evening.

We arrived at James's house. He had a room in the Grey's Inn Road area; this area was occupied with rooms for foreign students. Many houses were devoted to this. We walked up a couple of flights of stairs, and when we went, we found a medium-sized room with a fairly large window looking out onto the street. The room was moderately large, about twenty feet by sixteen feet. The walls had once been a cream color. Now with age there were tinges of green and brown. not exactly unpleasant, but not in any way a bright room. Short old curtains hung at the windows, curtains that had turned grey with age.

The best aspect of the room was that it had large, half-length windows that overlooked the street. There was s tall street lamp immediately below. There was no fireplace, but a gas heater had been installed. It was operated by putting a shilling into a meter.

The heater consisted of four asbestos-like bars with holes along them, and from these holes light and warmth emanated. There was also a single plate heater on a small stool. It also was coin-operated and allowed James to make tea. There was a kettle settled permanently on it. The only other fixture in the room was a small cupboard in which James kept a can of Carnation milk, Lipton's tea, and tins of biscuits. A milkman came by each day and left bottles of milk on the steps to the house for the tenants. James brought the milk up to this room. It was kept on the ledge outside the window or, if the weather was warm, hastily boiled on the hot plate to keep longer.

It was not an attractive room, and James had done nothing to brighten it. He seemed quite content with the way it looked. There were no pictures on the wall, framed reproductions, not any photographs at all. And the group found no objections to it. (Naipaul recalls that his visit to Maida Vale was to a rather dingy apartment.) On the floor there was well-worn brown linoleum. There was a good deal of dust in the room as well as at the windows. It was not exactly a dismal room, yet we, James and our small group, spent many hours there, so engrossed in our talk that we were scarcely aware of our surroundings.

There was not much furniture in the room. The major piece was the large round table where everyone sat. There was also a divan in one corner and a small bookcase. But books were not confined to that small space. There were books everywhere: books up the walls, books on the floor, books and papers on the table.

The other members of this assembled group were settled around the table. My impression that it was a first meeting was probably correct. The other members had met James only once or twice before. There were just eight of us. James introduced Esther and myself. We were the only women. The men already seated there greeted us warmly. I was introduced to two Oxford students, Jack Whittaker and a young man who had taken the pseudonym of Charles Sumner. Both were old friends. There was also a student at L. S. E., a Canadian named Earle Birney. There was also a worker, Arthur Ballard, a carpenter, who was to become important in the movement and also a young Indian named Roy. Later, I brought in three friends from London University. One was an engineer working for a big engineering company. (He became a shop steward, so he kept us informed of trade union matters from inside.) Not sitting at the table but standing in a corner or moving, from time to time, from one place to another around the room, was an Indian named Gupta. He never seemed to take part in any of the sessions, either on that day or any future day, but he was there often, almost daily. I was told by James that his father had a very large export business of jute in India and was a very wealthy man; that Gupta had a large allowance, but because of a restriction visa could not take part in any political groups or meetings. He was a tall, somewhat plump ivory-faced man, very genial. He was, all the time I knew him, a close friend of James. It is my impression, or it became my impression later, he was supporting James. Since James thought he was devoting his life to a cause, he had no bad feelings about taking money from people; he lived modestly and felt that other people could, if they were interested, contribute to the cause to which he was going to devote his life.

James started to tell us about Trotsky. Everyone later was to call him, or refer to him as the "Old Man." Obviously all the people in the room were acquainted with Trotsky's fame and all his works.

Since I was to be so closely associated with James for some years, I should tell about my own political background up until that time. I came from a conservative family, except for my eldest brother who called himself a Socialist. The family did not take him seriously, and he was not a serious person. He had been in the First World War, had been wounded, and had become thoroughly disillusioned. This was the basis of his new philosophy, but he never seriously acted a part in the furthering of his principles. I had always intended to be a writer. I thought I would be one of a new wave of women writers, such as Katherine Mansfield or Virginia Woolf. More particularly, I was to be a new Katherine Mansfield, because at that time I was only writing short stories. To illustrate my political ignorance, when at University College, London, there was railway strike, part of a General Strike. Some of the boys with whom a group of us young women were going out, were very amused because they were asked, at very high pay, to learn quickly, how to run London's underground trains. When they got their first and last pay, after nine days, we all went out and celebrated in Soho. I had no thought of the men who were striking. I considered it, as did these friends, something of a lark and did not look into the problem in any way. I was completely apolitical at that time.

A few years later, when I was married, all that changed. Because of new friends, my husband and I often used to visit flats in Hampstead and Chelsea and elsewhere in which there was always a great deal of political discussion. In particular, there was one apartment, or rather studio, in Chelsea rented by Gerry and Lee Bradley. I understood that they were Communists. At all of the parties we went to then there were always Communists. They were part of the environment, as it were, at that period.

Gerry told me at the time that one of the dreariest things of belonging to the Communist Party was having to read *The Daily Worker*. It was so dull and so full of wrong information. He also gave me some pamphlets about Trotsky. I became very interested then, and from that moment on started to read this literature and began to understand the causes of the political fight that existed around Trotsky. Gerry Bradley also used to go to Hyde Park, which has a corner where anybody can get up on a soapbox and orate about anything he wants. Often, my husband and I would go to the park to hear Gerry and to hear the other speakers, some of whom were Irish patriots who wanted Ireland for the Irish.

Gerry too felt Ireland should be for the Irish; that Britain would continue to have trouble until she gave the whole of Ireland freedom; that otherwise, there would always be bloodshed; that the English minority could easily be guaranteed all necessary civil liberties and safeguards.

Despite these happenings, however, it had somehow or the other, not occurred to me that they were Trotskyists, who were working within the Communist Party to try to overturn its position in regard to Stalin and to put the true facts on the Russian situation to the party. I really do not understand how I missed the implication. Perhaps it was because we went to many other parties such as that at the flat of Irene Rathbone. These were always sherry parties, so not very costly. People would drink and discuss all topics. Irene was a cousin of Basil Rathbone, the actor, and he often came to the parties. She herself was what was then being called a "Social Creditor." These people had some idea that if the banking system was fundamentally changed, then everything in the world would turn out very pleasantly. Of course, people who were followers of Trotsky and Stalin did not take the Social Creditors very seriously. And of course, too, at that time, there were the Fascists, followers of Oswald Mosley, and also supporters of Hitler and Hitler's ideas.

So you had a great variety of opinions at these various parties to which we used to go, parties that were often given by artists and writers, who were themselves either political or apolitical. I cannot imagine any such groups or any such freedom of speech in the United States. Or let me say, that I never encountered any such wealth of ideas from far right to far left being vaunted in any of the parties that I later went to in the States. Of course, sometimes it happened that these discussions turned into shouting matches; but on the whole, English people can get into diverse discussions and views without coming to blows.

This party period of which I write, the early thirties (1930–1932) must have been two or three years before I met James. Then I had a very serious attack of the flu and was in bed with a high temperature. I remember Gerry Bradley sent me a copy of Trotsky's *History of the Russian Revolution*. I became excited about it, and my temperature must have gone much higher. By the time I had finished the book, I was a convinced Trotskyist. I had become overnight deeply interested in his political struggle. It is a most memorable book. I think of it along with the great anarchist Kropotkin's *History of the French Revolution*.

Both are outstanding books, brilliantly written, and in Trotsky's case, not only written with passion, but also with wit. When I went to James's group, therefore, I really was a convinced Trotskyist with some reading background of not only Trotsky's major work, but also of a great many of his pamphlets that the Bradleys had given me. It was an intellectual gathering. We all sat around James's table and talked politics. Certainly CLR was the main contributor, but we were all, at that time, equally familiar with the works of Trotsky. Lenin and Marx were to come later. We discussed as equals. For James, it was as new to him as it was to us. He had done none of this reading in Trinidad.

This book is the story of my relationship during those years and in later years with C. L. R. James. Naturally, this relationship with CLR altered my relationship with my husband, though that had already been changing. When we had first gone to live in Hampstead Garden Suburb, we had engaged a young *au pair* girl from Germany. She was to help with the household chores but was to be treated as one of the family. My husband ensured this by sleeping with her a couple of times. The girl went back to Germany for a holiday. I should not have countenanced her return to our house, by my husband had assured me it was a momentary madness and that he truly loved me. When the girl returned, she had been caught up, while at home, in the enthusiasm for Hitler. She came back wearing a Nazi button. My husband, being a Jew, promptly put her on the next plane back to Germany. This must have been late 1932 or early 1933, before Hitler actually came to power.

Neither Dr. Heiger nor my husband joined James's group, though Dr. Heiger, too busy with cancer research, contributed money. Inevitably then, with my preoccupation with the group, I no longer went to parties with my husband; our interest had diverged. My husband did, however, keep a continued interest in the movement. He also designed the format for our small news sheet and often helped me with the layouts when it appeared.

James was a Trotskyist by the time I met him. So were the others around the table. I later learned that there had been three Trotskyist groups in London. But I cannot visualize James's being a follower in any other person's group. He would have to be the leader. So he had formed his own.

On one occasion, James brought up the idea that we should at least start a pamphlet or bulletin to put forth our views; a paper that we hoped we could sell not only to working-class people, but also at places such as Hyde Park corner, where people gathered. Everybody thought this was an excellent idea. James said we would all have to contribute to the funding for it.

James had asked if we had among us anyone who could devote full-time with him to publish the paper. I immediately said I would, because before that time I had been a journalist.

After finishing my course in journalism at University College, London, my first job was assistant editor of the *Nursery World*. It was at that time edited by a good reporter who had come over from the *News Chronicle*. The paper was published in Fleet Street in the house of Benn Brothers. Dorothy Sayers was one of their authors. I met her on several occasions. They also published a number of trade magazines. The *Nursery World* was one of these. It had been slanted to nannies; that is, nurses in private households who were looking after small children. It carried serial love stories and inferior-type articles. My editor was slowly changing it, and I helped her in making it a paper for new young middle-class mothers who no longer were able to afford nannies for their children. It had intelligent articles on the modern theory of raising children at that time. In general, she reshaped the magazine. Through her, too, I got a number of special articles to write for most of the Fleet Street Papers. I wrote for the *News Chronicle, Evening Standard, Daily Express, Sunday Express, and Daily Mirror*. I never got to write for *The Times*, but I did also book reviews for the BBC's periodical, *The Listener*. When my editor left the job, I was given the job of editor.

I was immensely interested, fairly recently listening to that delightful series about *Rumpole* on television, that a young woman lawyer said, when she found herself pregnant, "I will have to start buying *The Nursery World*," so it would seem that *The Nursery World* is still being published.

An incident that happened while I was with Sir Ernest Benn & Co., was that his son and his nephew accosted me in one of the corridors one day and asked me whether I would like to play the lead part in some theatrical production they were proposing to do. I was tempted, but I was at that time writing my first novel, and I suppressed the temptation because I thought it would take me away from my writing. I suggested that they use my secretary, a pretty, blond, young woman. They did so—and she later became the wife of one of them, and it is her son, Tony Benn, who is now in Parliament and is considered the "bad boy" in British politics.

At this time, too, I did a series of articles for *The Evening Standard* on some new schools. Until then, all schools were segregated, but there were one or two experimental schools being started. This included one that Bertrand and Dora Russell were running at his house in Sussex. I went to see him. He was extremely cordial, surprisingly so because he had never been sympathically handled by the press. I went with a photographer of *The Evening Standard,* and we took photographs. I listened to all he had to say on education and felt that if I had only been in the hands of someone who had a similar philosophy to his on education, my own development would have been greater. This is getting a little far away from James, but it was an interesting part of my development.

Also, Russell had already met Trotsky, when he had just returned from visiting the Red Army at the front. He writes of him: "Very Napoleonic expression, . . . bright eyes, military bearing, lightning intelligence, magnetic personality. Exceedingly good looking . . . would be irresistible to women. . . . I felt a vein of gay, good humor, as long as he was not crossed in any way. Ruthless, not cruel. Admirable wavy hair. Vanity even greater than love of power."

After having had that first visit, Bertrand Russell was kind enough to ask me down for several weekends. I remember being a very shy young woman among his weekend guests, where there would be people like Sylvia Pankhurst or her sister, Lancelot Hogben, and Julian Huxley. Not that they talked necessarily on a high intellectual level, obviously they talked of quite mundane things, but I was definitely overwhelmed by being in such company. Bertrand Russell also would ask me to tea in his tower at the top of the house. The tower had four-sided windows, so that you could look across the country from every side. We would have China tea. He told me about himself; about some of his travels; how he liked China, disliked Japan, and that he had already been to Russia and did not have any sympathy with the Communist regime. We also took long walks together, and I shall always be grateful to him for giving me what was a minor but further education for a young woman.

Bertrand Russell was a pacifist and had been in prison during the First World War because of his views. He told me that when he went to jail that he had taken a Bible, and inside the cover he had hidden a razor blade in case he would not be able to take the experience of being shut up. He was also later to be advocating trial marriage; that is, people should live together for a short while until they were sure they were suitable to each other, because so many marriages ended in divorce or unhappiness on both sides. He wrote a book, *Companionate Marriage* in which these ideas were expressed, only to obtain great condemnation for subverting youth, both in Great Britain and the United States, and even in the universities. Russell would later lend his name to a British Committee for the Defense of Leon Trotsky.

I had also been an assistant editor on London *Vogue*. This was in the early thirties, and it is surprising that here in this smart woman's magazine, no married woman was allowed to be on the staff. It is really incredible to think that such was the situation. Actually, I was married and had to hide the fact and was amused by the other editors, who were all somewhat older that I was, who felt that *Vogue* would be a wonderful launching pad for a "good marriage" for me, because we rubbed shoulders with society people, people in the theater and the arts, and people in various prominent spheres.

When James called for journalistic help, I could say that I had experience. As a journalist, I could put a magazine together, do pasteups and layouts, deal with a printer, and of course, write. I am not sure at that time whether we started with a monthly and then tried to move it to twice a month. I think, however, that in all, we only published a few issues as specific crises arose.

I think James saw me in the role of a faithful Krupskaya to his role of Lenin. He writes: "We have an unforgettable picture of Krupskaya supervising the duplication of letters, scrupulous over every comma, so that the Bolshevik agitators might be able to put Lenin's precise ideas clearly before the eager masses."

In these early days when I worked regularly with James, his novel *Minty Alley* was published. I was there when the proofs came, and I helped with the proofreading and editing. I have an inscription of *Minty Alley* with his many thanks for all my help. I gave it to Profesor Robert Hill, who is C. L. R. James's literary executor.

However, what I considered much more important and far more interesting was when he started writing *The Black Jacobins*. This is the story of Toussaint L'Ouverture and the rebellion in Haiti against both the Creoles and the whites there, and finally against Napoleon's forces that were sent against him. I used to go to the British Museum and help with some of the research. It was perhaps James's finest book and is considered one of the most authoritative ones by those interested in Haiti. Yet oddly, as far as I know, he never visited Haiti.

After the book was published, James decided to make the book into a play, and when it was finished, he got his friend Paul Robeson to take the leading part. This was fascinating because it meant we went to the theater each day and saw all the rehearsals, and I became quite friendly with Robeson, a very powerful man, with a wonderful voice, and a man of great character. He, as is known, had accepted a Communist position, but he and James could still have a close relationship.

I had not realized until fairly recently that my family knew what I was doing and disapproved. But my younger brother later reminded me that I had taken him behind the scenes and into Robeson's dressing room and how impressed he was by that great actor.

There was some talk of James's taking part in the play, but I knew that was not really seriously considered. Unfortunately, the play was not a success. The book, however, remains a major work on the Haitian revolution and is quoted in all sources about that Caribbean island. I think that James very much identified himself with Toussaint L'Ouverture, who had not in the beginning aligned himself with the revolution. He had been the coachman of a family, a family to whom he was attached, and he had by his own efforts educated himself.

Being devoted to the wife of his slave owner. Toussaint L'Ouverture took her in the coach safely to the southern part of the island. It was a gesture of personal chivalry. Not until he had rescued her and seen that she was safe did he return home and join the revolution. James admired gallantry in politics and on the cricket field.

L'Ouverture once was asked by a frightened young black slave how it was possible to overcome the white people. Toussaint L'Ouverture took a jar. He put black beans in and filled it almost to the top. Then he spread some white beans over them, shook the jar, and said to the boy, "See, they have almost disappeared."

This attitude James felt applied to Africa, in particular to South Africa, where the whites stood with ironclad shoes on the shoulders of the blacks. It was what made him so particularly vehement about the war against Abyssinia by Mussolini then still continuing, and also in the fights for independence in Africa.

The Black Jacobins was translated and published in France. Also, the play was used as the basis for an opera, *Toussaint,* by the National Opera Company in London a number of years later. It is also the only full-length book about blacks that C. L. R. James ever wrote.

Since I worked closely with James, I met his few black friends.

One was George Padmore, who had been a boyhood friend of his in Trinidad. They had not been to the same schools but had spent many summer holidays together. Padmore had been prominent as a Communist and had been to Moscow; but in 1935, he broke away from the Stalinists. Then there was another friend from Trinidad, Eric Williams. For several years, James had been a teacher, and one of his pupils was Williams. Eric Williams was later to become prime minister of Trinidad. When James went back to his native land, twenty-five years after leaving it, he and Williams became political antagonists. Another friend from the Caribbean, Norman Manley, was to become premier of Jamaica. His son, Michael Manley, also became prime minister there. He has an English wife. A few African men, who would become leaders, also came to see us. In 1935, James was to help Marcus Garvey's wife publish *African Opinion*.

There were other visitors who came because they were interested in our political stance. A serious enquirer was George Orwell, of 1984 fame. Since he was so vehemently against Stalin's regime in the Soviet Union, he read and approved the literature we had. In the end, he decided he wanted to continue as a writer and not get mixed up in politics.

He had been in Spain helping in the fight against the Fascists. Mary Low, who had been there too at the time must also have visited us, for James was to write a "blurb" about her Red Spanish Diary, but I do not remember her. For me, the many exciting discussions with James's friends and visitors were very stimulating, and I took part in them all, for they happened mostly not when the group met but when we were alone together.

So began my close association with CLR—I, a young bourgeois woman whose aims, until then, had been to be a first-class literary writer, was pushed into a revolutionary ambiance. But it was an experience that for me, too, would color my political perspective for a lifetime.

When I started writing my own books at last, they were written from the perspective of those views I had learned in James's London group. They were about the Caribbean, but not about Trinidad and the English islands there, but about Puerto Rico and the Spanish Caribbean. They were written mostly from a political viewpoint, not a literary one.

2
The Marxist Group

THE TROTSKYIST MOVEMENT STARTED IN ENGLAND, AS IT DID IN other European countries, in 1927. It also started naturally within the Communist parties, since they were the ones most interested in what was happening in Russia. The Communists could not at first believe the news that Trotsky was in disfavor, as people in the Soviet Union could not. They, as the Russian people, had very little knowledge of what was happening. Lenin had died in 1924, and Trotsky was a man who had stood beside Lenin. Trotsky forged the Red Army that was able to conquer both the White Army and the armies that the Allies sent to help them. It was a prodigious feat based on the fortitude and faith of the Russian workers and peasants who made up the military. He did not hesitate to take under his command officers of the Imperial Army who were sympathetic to his aims.

Trotsky had been chosen by the people, as early as the Revolution of 1905, to be their representative in the Soviets of that time. He was a magnificent orator, holding crowds spellbound. His name and that of Lenin's had been linked closely in the revolution, almost as if the two names were one. Now he was in disgrace. How had that come about? Everyone was mystified and puzzled.

The basic fact was that Trotsky was an intellectual and a statesman. He had not the wiliness and shrewdness to compete with Stalin, the politician. Stalin had, during the years as general secretary of the party, put people loyal to him in key positions, so that in any showdown in the party, he would have the votes in the central committee. His first act was to not let Trotsky, who was in ill health in the south, hear the news of Lenin's death. People asked: Why did not Trotsky attend the funeral? It was the first seed of distrust sewn. Trotsky, returning to Moscow, should have summoned a great crowd and in anger told them he had not been informed by Stalin. From the first moment, Stalin would have been put on the defensive. Then, when he was deprived of this command of the army,

Trotsky should have let the people know of his outrage. When he was thus deprived and placed in a lower position, which was published nonetheless as being a higher one, again Trotsky should have gone to the people.

Unfortunately, Trotsky was misguided enough to believe that he had to accept party discipline in the interest of the Soviet State. As demotion followed demotion, opposition arose to Stalin. Still Trotsky did not seriously fight. Yet he had known that Lenin in his "Last Testament" had described Stalin "as too peppery a cook to be in charge." The testament was withheld until long after Stalin's death, and not until the coming of Nikita Khrushchev was it to be made public, and he began also to open other cracks in the structure of Stalin's Communist Party.

Little by little, Stalin destroyed the Left Opposition in the country. Eventually, he brought to trial many of the old Bolshevik leaders who had been stalwart supporters of Lenin. Then, he undertook first, the expulsion of Trotsky and then, his indictment, with a trial that would have world coverage.

The Communist Party of Great Britain supported Stalin's new policy of "socialism in a single country" and thus in reality overthrew the old policy of revolutionary internationalism. Stalin was also shrewd enough to get the Communist Third International to make the first expulsions. The first victim of the suppression of the Left Opposition was Boris Souvarine of the French Communist Party. In September 1927, Trotsky was expelled from the Communist International. Many of those who were to be first used by Stalin for the expulsion of others, in turn in later years, were to find themselves expelled, imprisoned, or executed.

So within the Communist Party in Britain, there grew Trotsky dissidents early, who felt they were not hearing the truth. At first they were tolerated then as the pressure from the Kremlin grew, they were expelled. A few Trotskyists went into the Independent Labour Party (ILP). There was a breakaway group in Glasgow, and another, calling itself The Marxist League, in London.

So there were a handful of Trotsky supporters on the scene before James appeared. It was the last group that James must have been in touch with on his return to London late in 1932. He himself began to read the literature and became a convinced Trotskyist.

We were a very small group, though I think that James had met with other Trotskyists and encouraged some into the group he was forming. I repeat I cannot see him at any time as a follower, but only as a leader. He had to have his own group of which he was the head. In the beginning we always met at his place in Heathecote

Street in Bloomsbury, and mostly on Sundays or two or three evenings a week. Some of the people such as Arthur Ballard, who was a workingman, and the others, had other duties they needed to perform during the day.

Evenings and Sundays were the best times for us. Except for the dinner party at which we first met, we never convened again at the Heiger's house. We produced a bulletin called *Fight* on which James and I worked. The group formed the editorial committee, making the decisions about who should write which articles. It was published infrequently, and it was probably only four pages, but we published it when we had money. James wanted to produce a paper because the other existing Trotskyist groups already had their own papers. The Balham Group had their *Red Flag*. The Chelsea Group, to which the Bradleys belonged, produced the *Militant,* and later together with a youth group, the *Youth Militant.* Our small effort in no way compared with either of these already well-established small newspapers. Besides, James had neither the money nor the knowledge to produce the paper. This was left to me because I alone among the group had already had the experience. We covered all the current British political topics and also all that was happening in Europe. As far as I know, none of those papers that we printed ever survived.

There has been some confusion about the journal *Fight* in recent years. Anna Grimshaw writes that James conceived and developed the journal as if it were a great conception. James suggested that we needed to have a paper, but that was obvious to us all. Instead of James, another member of the group might well have done so. We all fully agreed. (Grimshaw was referring to the later *Fight,* which was not brought out until 1937, after we had joined the ILP. The Trotskyists publishing *Red Flag* suggested we merge our small effort with their larger one, but it was decided the name of our paper should be used.) Robert J. Alexander also makes the same mistake regarding what was the second *Fight,* when he mistakenly suggests that "James had managed to produce on his own initiative,

---

Only of the later, longer *Fight,* which was more substantial and which went to about twelve or more pages, are copies still available. But those early sheets that we produced seemed not to have survived from those many years that have passed since their issue. The later one was a combination *Red Flag,* a bigger paper, and ours, resulting in a different *Fight,* and when all three groups following Trotsky's suggestion entered into the left wing of the Labour Party, the Independent Labour Party, headed by Fenner Brockway.

and which called openly for the Fourth International, the new journal which was called *Fight*."

At that meeting at which the new *Fight* was established, James was not even present: A copy of the minutes is still available. *Red Flag's* managing editor became the managing editor of the new *Fight*. He was a man of substance; either then or later he was a member of Parliament. He saw to the production and distribution of the paper and found the money for it. For our small effort, we had little money. James had none, and the others of us in the group were not particularly well-off. We had never had the resources to fund a good-sized media for the expression of our views. The MP"s wife became general secretary, and I was voted editor. Since I had worked so closely together on our earlier effort, I suggested that CLR be brought in as coeditor. Everyone agreed. No names appeared on the front page about the editorial staff. A third editor was co-opted, as well as other people to help with the day-to-day work.

James had kept us apart from the other Trotskyist groups. Until we entered the ILP we did not know they existed. There were actually two other groups existing in London when James decided to form his own group. Besides the Marxist League, there was the Balham Group, which included Reg Groves and Harry Wicks. We met both men and became well acquainted with them only when we entered the ILP. Both had been working within the Communist Party as had Gerry and Lee Bradley. Groves had been working as an organizer as early as the general strike, while Harry Wicks had spent three years at the Lenin School in Moscow. The Balham Group was already established in 1931, and they were already in touch with Trotsky and also the Socialist Workers Party (SWP) in New York. These also were people James must have met with when he decided to form his own group rather than to join them.

When we were in the ILP and the Fourth International was formed, with the fusion of our group with the larger group, the paper *Fight* of which everyone writes was initiated. Why they chose the name of our paper and not that of the *Red Flag's* I do not remember. James did not himself conceive it. His role was only one of the three coeditors.

Robert J. Alexander, *International Trotskyism* (Durham: Duke University Press, 1991), states that the first organized group in Great Britain to take a position in defense of Trotsky and to seek to interpret his ideas was the Marxist League, which was formed in 1929 to 1930. He gives the names of people who would play a part in the Trotskyist movement. Among the names are Lee and Gerry Bradley. That I never met them again after they had given me Trotsky's works must be because they later went into the Labour Party when we were going into the ILP.

Alexander makes the mistake also of suggesting that it was James's idea that, with the breakdown of the ILP, all the groups should fuse and go into the Labour Party. It was Trotsky's suggestion. James *opposed* it. He wanted all those dissidents who also opposed the idea, to form a new group outside *under his leadership* when he came back from three months in the United States. It was from this point that James began his first break with Trotsky.

In those early days, I realized if I was going to write for our bulletin and keep up with the other members of the group, I had to increase my knowledge of British and world affairs. Enthusiastically, I began to read a whole new library of books about Marxism and world politics. James did the same reading. It was new to us both.

I began also, to collect my own library. We bought books from a friend of James's a bookseller named Charlie Lahr, who had a store close by. He often gave discounts to the group's members. I like to have my own books because I have a habit of underlining sentences, marking paragraphs, and making notes in the margins. In the blank pages at the back of the book, I also write my impressions of it and make points for or against those raised in the pages. It helps me to go back to my books, at any time, and quickly find passages I want to quote or to remember.

In the group we read the various books that Trotsky wrote—the German situation was then of most importance. We discussed the books and the Trotsky general line of the moment. These books included *The Revolution Betrayed* and *The Only Road*. They greatly helped us in understanding events in Europe and the totally wrong policies of Stalin. I think we would have been lost without them.

Soon, Trotsky was in constant communication with us, sending us a letter, I imagine, about once a month, when any particular subject of importance came up, or when any new political event occurred. We were also, after a while, in touch with the Trotskyists in the States. Max Eastman, James Cannon, and Max Schachtman, for instance, wrote us regularly, and we sold their periodical the *Militant* along with our own bulletin.

The group had so much to discuss. As I have written, in the parties I went to in my apolitical days, there was a cloud, a sense of doom, a sense of inevitability of the coming war; the main political divisions ran high. Hitler's power was rising fast, and most people saw him as the threat to peace.

It was the German situation that we discussed mostly and that occupied us in so much of the coming period at James's place. James pointed out that the Fascists had taken over the Workers' Party and had added Socialism to its name, so that the party's name became National Socialist Workers' Party, abbreviated to "Nazi." It may be remembered that Mussolini also started as a Socialist, dropped out of the party, but offered to the people a campaign program of progressive reform, which, of course, he did not fulfill when he headed the government.

This was the period when the Communists were calling Social Democrats "Social Fascists" in Germany, Britain, and France. It was a suicidal strategy, splitting the workers especially in Germany; pitting workers against workers. In one prominent election, the Communists had incredibly even voted with the Fascists. The Socialists were the only ones fighting the Fascists in the streets. How heatedly our small group expressed their disgust of the Communists and how warmly we supported the workers.

Not until the opportunity of unity was passed, and the danger at last realized, did the Communists make one of their usual zigzags: the Socialist parties now became brothers; indeed, they opened their arms to everyone in a united front against Hitler as the fear grew that Hitler would march against the Soviet Union.

The popular front that the Communists now called for, was not a union of the workers against war, but was a call to all to support the war against Fascism. They had finally called for unity to fight against Fascism in Germany in the country where it had grown, and where it could and should have been stopped.

Trotsky wanted the Soviet Union to be defended in case of war, because he felt that though it was a deformed socialist state, it was still a socialist state. This view was not unanimously accepted. Indeed, later James was to make his final break with Trotsky, on this very point. CLR felt and others with him, that Stalin had to be overthrown and a new revolution occur before the Soviet Union could break the newly imposed chains of its entrenched and privileged bureaucracy. It was Stalin's betrayal of the revolution that would lead, finally, in 1994, to the ultimate dissolution of the Soviet Union. (It is incredible to me that Russians in Leningrad today should be prepared to replace the name with the old one of St. Petersburg. Peter the Great built that beautiful city, the "Venice of the North," by the terrible expenditure of millions of lives of Russian peasants and workers.)

By this time, Hitler had begun the extermination of his opponents and his first preparation for a war of expansion in Europe. Trotsky had been writing of the disastrous results of splitting workers throughout this period. James then enthusiastically supported

Trotsky, and all the members of the group discussing the situation around the table gave their support.

I had seen the Nazis in Germany, in the summer of 1932. My husband and I went for a holiday by car, through Europe to go to the Salzburg Festival. I remember at first, in the Bavarian Forest, we saw the Nazi Youth. They had looked quite innocuous; not any different from Boy Scouts in England and the States. But then when we passed through some of the Bavarian villages, it was dismaying to see banners stretched across the entrances to the villages stating, "Juden Nicht Wielkommen." Yet these people were still quite friendly and met us with a greeting "Greuz Gott," as we passed. But we came to a large town, I forget which one it was, and our hotel room had a balcony. Looking straight down the street from that balcony was a wide square. There were big advertisements everywhere for a Hitler rally that night. We then were appalled to see the tremendous crowds with their almost frenzied, delirious support of Hitler. We could hear, even though it must have been a good three-fourths of a mile away, the loud cries of "Heil Hitler." They were mostly middle-class people and not workers themselves. In fact, the workers had begun to fight the Nazis in the street. The Stalinist policy was to call them, if they were not within the Communist Party or sympathizers, "Social Fascists," and to give no help in their fight: no Jews, unless they were in the workers' parties, helped either. The scene we had witnessed from our hotel balcony stayed with us as a very vivid memory for years: that frenzied crowd had been a very chilling, frightening sight.

On a lighter note, as we were in Bodensee and were walking near a fountain with a statue, two Nazi soldiers started to walk towards us—my husband was a Jew—we stood very rigid. He was terrified; for myself, I was terrified for him. But actually the young men came up to us and asked us only to take their photographs against the statue.

When we got into Austria, we found the pro-Hitler sentiment very high. In Vienna, we saw Karl Marxhof's (house) with great holes in the walls that earlier had been made when big guns were turned against his working-class apartment house. We also found that the wealthier Jews were not against the Nazis. They did not believe at that time, that they themselves would be vulnerable. They felt that the Nazis would want their wealth, and that they would be safe. In the end, of course, or toward the end, they recognized the danger and most of the wealthiest of them were able to escape, mostly to the States. Among the mountaineers in Austria were young men wearing white knee-high stockings. The white stockings represented their adherence to the Hitler regime.

After some time, Trotsky suggested that our group and the other groups should enter the ILP and "bore from within," as it were, as the Stalinists were doing. They were trying to take over what had been Left Wing of the Labour Party. The ILP, as well as the Labour Party itself ran parliamentary candidates, so that it was in touch with the people by canvasing and through its own newspaper, *The New Leader*. We would not be allowed to enter the ILP with our own paper. Our group was very small, though it had grown larger. I myself introduced three new members. I do not believe it ever numbered many, certainly never more than twenty. However, we split, so that the few outside could be "purists" and put out a bulletin with our particular point of view, which those inside the ILP could use and distribute among ILP members. Fenner Brockway, its leader, was quite glad when we and the other Trotskyists entered the party, because he was coping then with the Stalinists who were also trying to take over. He had some defenders in all of us, and he became friendly with James and me and the others. James also, through the ILP, was offered a number of speaking engagements that were helpful for us. I was acting as a sort of aide-de-camp to James. So on occasions, I would speak at halls when James, for one reason or another, could not go. He gave me various pointers on speaking. I was always extremely nervous before I got a platform, though I gather this is usual, but when I started speaking I became quite passionate. However, there were moments when my mind suddenly went blank. James suggested that I always have written slips of paper with the next subject or the next point of view I planned to cover. He took his with him, and I followed his example: six or eight sheets of paper with topics listed in large lettering. If I found myself drying up, I only had to look down to see another subject to talk on. By that time, James had become a fairly well-known speaker in our political circles; but only in our circles, not nationwide.

Today, in 1995, I see the United States moving toward Fascism and the people approving of that move. There is a curtailing of civil rights, the extension of the death penalty, which means more deaths of blacks and Hispanics, the rising tide of racism in every sphere, and applause of military might destroying thousands of innocent people such as in Panama and the Gulf War, so long as those thousands are not North Americans. It is in the country where the beginning signs of Fascism are seen, that Fascism must be fought, not in later wars. It was in Oklahoma, in 1995, that the United States saw the results of the ultraright militias that had been growing all over the country. These militias are at present antigovernment, but if

He was a charismatic speaker. He tended to talk in friendly person-to-person terms, until those moments when his voice rose in passion and he made his most cogent points. On the other hand, I was never able to achieve this close relationship with an audience. The moment I looked down from the platform and saw all those individual people, I assumed some might be hostile, and I was lost. I could only speak over their heads into space. I recognized that this was the difference between a rousing speaker such as CLR and a merely acceptable one as myself. James always asked Earle Birney for a report on how I had "made out" when I substituted for him.

He himself spoke at one meeting in Trafalgar Square, standing up beside the stone lions, to thousands of people in an antiwar rally in the late thirties. It was the ILP that gave James the opportunity to develop as a speaker. This was his talent: a progression from being a born talker.

With group meetings and discussions, with attending James's speeches, with helping to edit and publish *Fight* life was very full. Once we entered into the ILP, James also wrote for the *New Leader*, the ILP paper, and *Controversy*, the interparty paper to which I also contributed. James and my name appeared occasionally on the front-page box of the contributors.

It was through Fenner Brockway that James was introduced to the publisher who commissioned him in 1936 to write *World Revolution*. Several of us in the group helped him by clipping newspapers and periodicals with relevant items that he needed and by finding other source material. Harry Wicks, an older man who had been one of the first dissidents within the Communist Party, also gave him considerable assistance.

The thirties was a period of great political happenings throughout the world. There was the Italian war against Abyssinia, the Spanish Civil War, the Chinese Revolution, the rise to power of Hitler, the Moscow Trials. Trotsky wrote brilliantly on all these momentous events. He provided answers, suggested correct strategies. We were all, including James, his loyal followers.

Our small, group though now in the ILP, still sat around James's bed-sitting room table, just a handful of us, enjoying one another's companionship ardently discussing political topics, with James, of course having the lion's share of the talk. We kept up our personal adherence to Trotsky through these regular meetings that were still held at James's rooming house. We had all become close comrades.

---

they grow enough, they could try to take over the country as Hitler did from the democratic Weimar Republic.

By this time, Charles Sumner, who had not actually left us, was working to form a Committee almost by himself for the Defense of Trotsky. After the trials and executions of the Bolsheviks, Stalin put Leon Trotsky on trial in absentia in the dock of world opinion. They used so may terrible lies and deceptions on this man who was one of the most brilliant in the century, and who was, with Lenin, one of the foremost leaders of the two Russian revolutions.

Charles set about getting a number of people, not necessarily political people, who would be glad to look into the accusations and find them false. Unfortunately, he named the group Committee for the Defense of Leon Trotsky. The name was wrong because it meant anyone who was asked to join was already on the side of Trotsky. Bernard Shaw for instance, who was interested and had some correspondence with Charles, pointed out that if the judges were to be fair and their opinion to be considered by public opinion, then they had to be people who had not already taken sides. Charles worked on this almost by himself, and he got permission from a number of prominent people to let their names be used on his committee. He was in constant communication with Trotsky and wrote to him both in French and in English. Also, Trotsky asked him how his followers were now being active, for they were once again disbursed both in the Labour Party and the ILP, and still some functioning outside of both. This correspondence was made much easier for Charles since he had met Trotsky when he was in exile in Norway and had also met his wife there. So each knew the other as they corresponded.

Charles suggested to the "Old Man" that James's group suffered in some measure from "infantile leftism" (Lenin had written a pamphlet *Left Wing Communism: An Infantile Disorder,* which made it a current phrase at the time). James Cannon, coming from the United States to meet with us, reported back that the British Trotskyists were being philosophers instead of revolutionaries. We were all inexperienced young people, that is our particular group was. The other groups were more sophisticated politically.

Our small group did think in those years before the war, whose inevitability we foresaw, that in its aftermath, there would be revolution after revolution throughout the world and that it would also happen in Great Britain. The Communist Party was of the same opinion. Harry Pollitt, the Communist leader, was also proclaiming its coming, its inevitability. James believed that the coming war of 1939, would bring the realization to people of all nations, that the dying and destruction were never in their interests, and that they would rise up against those that led them to die in wars neither of their choosing nor their interests. This was the correct Trotskyist view.

"A bold stand for internationalism at the beginning of the war would have enormous significance in every country," James would write in *World Revolution*. When that war came against Hitler, this did not happen. Meanwhile, the Communists, by their policies of calling fellow workers Social Fascists, had helped to see that it did not happen. Incredibly, even Stanley Baldwin, the overthrower of a king, was saying during the Abyssinian War, "that in a new war, the common people would rise up in wrath and sweep governments away."

James also wrote in *World Revolution:* "Whenever a Socialist society is established in the world, its armies might conceivably be defeated by hostile powers, but the restoration of Capitalism is impossible." Yet, as I write in 1996, capitalism is being restored in the Soviet Union, and Yeltsin is changing the socialist society into a market economy. This has already happened, or is in the process of happening, in Poland, East Germany, Czechoslovakia, and Hungary, which were all Socialist societies.

James continued: "Even before the revolutions of 1848, Marx and Engels had foretold an inevitable breakdown in the economic system of capitalism," and "The bourgeois system is no longer able to cope with the abundance of the wealth it creates." Though there still may be a "rise and fall" of the United States empire, as some writers foretell, despite its military might, because of its unsolved social problems and its fantastic five trillion dollar debt, there does not appear to be, at this moment, any sign of a socialist revolution on the horizon. In fact, as I write today, it is the religious right wing that is coming to the forefront. Even to be a liberal, that is fair-minded, person is politically unacceptable to those in power. It is beginning to look like Hitler's days of prospering.

I suppose we, as a group, identified ourselves with Lenin in exile in Switzerland. But the situation in Russia was vastly different from that in Great Britain. In Russia, there had been a revolution in 1905, when Soviets were established. The peasants and workers were certain again to arise against all the oppression and misery they suffered. Lenin rightly believed that this spontaneous uprising, if it were not to be crushed, needed leadership.

In Great Britain, in the thirties, there was no such comparison. We were all young and idealistic. We felt our work could contribute to the time when we would see Socialism spreading, when the poor would not be starving, when the homeless were given shelter, when the unemployed would be guaranteed jobs. Most of all, we believed, we could help working people of all nations realize that they had no interest in fighting in imperialist wars, that in each nation they would be ready to join with the underclass of other nations. Workers of the world unite: It is the only way to peace.

How grand our dreams were. How they have all fallen.

However, it always pleases me now, to realize that the seeds we sowed developed in England and that now in the British Houses of Parliament there are Trotskyist members. There are Trotsky's groups, too, still spread all over the world from South Africa to Europe, to the Caribbean, though all still remain small. Trotsky is long dead, but his many books supply the basic policies to follow in any situation.

James's extensive work *World Revolution* at the time was dedicated to our Marxist group. His political existence depended on us. Rereading James's *World Revolution,* however, it is sad, no, tragic, to realize how high our hopes were then. James wrote: "The war will begin as a conflict between nations and nations. The end of it will be the beginning of an era of conflict between the rulers and ruled, in which all old deceptions suffered by the workers in central Europe, the bitterness and despair accumulated during the past twenty-five years, will find decisive expression in the working-classes striving for power." He wrote that this will happen elsewhere, too, in Great Britain and countries worldwide. He himself was later disillusioned, but not then. Then we were all so young.

I was in the group that held these beliefs then, and I, too, was intoxicated with the righteousness and certainty of our cause. This critique, fifty years later, of our failure correctly to understand the situation in Great Britain, does not take away from the fine analysis and power of James's book written in 1937.

In the years just preceding World War II, there was a sense of doom and gloom throughout the British Isles; people desperately wanted peace. But would they revolt before or after it? The answer is no. Yet the students at Oxford University cried: "We will not fight for King and Country." Earl Grey had an enormous mass following for his peace movement. But it was expressed in a general feeling, not with the concrete actions that should have been undertaken.

I remember a big demonstration for peace that took place in the Marble Arch, Hyde Park area. At one point, I was pushed over by the great rump of a big horse that a mounted policeman was riding, as part of the effort to break up the protesting citizens. Luckily, I only staggered and fell against a throng of other people. But I remember how terrifying it was to feel that one might be trampled by the horses; we who had been taught from childhood to look on the police as our friends. However, much he might be maligned later, when Chamberlain brought back his promise of "Peace in Our Time," the whole country heaved a deep sigh of relief.

Our Marxist group lasted till the end of 1938, when James left for the United States. The group, as such, more or less disintegrated, though as individuals some of us went on working within the Labour Party.

There was a first and only political rift between James and myself before he left for North America to which he had been invited by the SWP. The ILP was disintegrating. Some of the Trotskyist within it chose to join the Labour Party as Trotsky now suggested. The Communist Party had already abandoned the ILP; therefore, the only place to fight them was within the greater mass party. Trotsky felt that we should as a group, and with the other groups, follow suit. The ILP was then no longer affiliated with the Labour Party, and it was to the Labour Party that the mass of the workers belonged.

James disagreed in part. At first I went along with him. We had the majority on the editorial board of *Fight*. James wrote: "Without the revolutionary party there can be no hope for the workers of Britain." The group addressed this article to the ILP. "We therefore withdraw form the ILP and call all revolutionaries inside and outside to join us or collaborate with us in laying the foundation of a revolutionary party." James then was leaving the ILP to form his own group to which he called all Trotskyists to join. This call does not seem to be generally known.

Those within the Labour Party already responded that "believing as we do that the place for all revolutionaries at the present time is inside a mass party—the Labour Party—we can only deplore the actions of the Marxist Group' in forming an independent organization which has no real basis and must lead to their isolation from the mass of the politically conscious workers. We foresee the speedy collapse of this untimely experiment—the 'Marxist Group' does not represent the majority of the British Trotskyists."

Trotsky was fully supporting the idea of the grouping together of all British Trotskyists within the Labour Party. In fact, he had suggested it. On the other hand, James supported the grouping together of all the British Trotskyists, *but under his leadership,* in a revolutionary party. In later years, he was to abandon this position completely on the necessity of a revolutionary party, for which then he had stood so firmly.

Another point of contention in the group at this time was whether to vote for Labour candidates in the national elections. James felt his followers should not, but most of us disregarded his dictum and voted for Labour Party candidates. After he left for the States, I joined the Labour Party. Arthur Ballard went back into the ILP and became Secretary of the British Center against Imperialism. Also he managed to get the ILP to set up a Colonial Bureau for its 1939 conferences. The bureau was set up after James left.

Though most of the Trotskyist remained in the Labour movement, *our* group as such finally, more or less, came to an end with the departure of James for North America at the end of 1938.

James wrote very highly of Trotsky in his book *World Revolution*. But unfortunately, Trotsky had mildly criticized the book. Was this the reason that James at first differed, then broke with Trotsky and the Trotskyists? It could not have been easy for James to swallow Trotsky's assessment of his book. James had surely hoped for praise. Trotsky felt that James's book was undialectical: "It treated as fixed and set, processes that were still in flux." In particular, Trotsky did not agree that it was Stalin's express will and intention that Hitler should come to power in 1938 as James had suggested in his anti-Stalinist stance.

With all Trotskyists not coming to his support of a new group under his direction outside both the ILP and the Labour Party, James saw more of his friend and fellow Trinidadian George Padmore. After leaving the Communist Party, Padmore turned his attention to developing an independent socialist perspective on the colonial question, particularly that of Africa. James, too, turned his attention in the same direction. James and Padmore were brought together politically by the crisis and political mobilization brought about by the Italo-Ethiopian War of 1935–36. James produced a short pamphlet, *A History of Negro Revolt,* that was similar in many ways to Padmore's *Life and Struggles of Negro Toilers*.

Of that time, I believe I am the only one alive now who can give a true account of it.

It is sad and may now seem pathetic that the small group formed by James in London in the Thirties, sitting around that table in that dusty room could have hoped to have an effect not only in England, but with others internationally. It was not that we were intellectually

---

Even while Lenin lived, Trotsky was the most brilliant figure in Russia," "Trotsky had been the leading figure before the masses in Petrograd. He was the 'Man of October,'" "His organization of the Red Army had given him not only an international reputation but a vast popularity among peasants;" "He was the greatest orator in Europe," "His pamphlets appealed equally to professors and peasants."

arrogant but lost in the excitement and camaraderie to which only the young can perhaps aspire.

But how we talked. How excitedly we talked, and C. L. R. James, our leader, "the born talker," talked most of all. Yet being in that small group with such a man as James changed us all. We would go our separate ways later; still the mark of those days of our youth, when we discussed and discussed among ourselves, myself among my warm-hearted comrades, listening eagerly to C. L. R., that mark would never be lost to us in memory: those years when we had been not only so young in years but young in heart.

3
Background of World Events

IT IS NECESSARY TO KNOW THE POLITICAL BACKGROUND AGAINST which we young people were working in our group that revolved around C. L. R. James. These were years of great upheavals and wars in all of Europe. They had begun with the end of World War I and would extend with backswings to the start of World War II. Seeds sown at the end of one conflict inevitably led to the even more terrible conflict of the second, and to the lesser wars in years in between.

Many revolutionary movements arose all over Europe. After the 1917 revolution in Russia, Lenin and Trotsky hoped that the revolution in 1918 in Germany, led by Rosa Luxemburg and Karl Liebknecht would be successful. If this happened, Germany would provide the necessary industrial unit, and the USSR would have been the breadbasket for both. Should this have happened, the rise of Hitler would have been forestalled. Europe would have had a different shape; A different social environment would have been created. But the revolution was crushed.

After World War II, the successful Allied armies forged Croatia, Slovakia, Dalmatia, and Serbia into the single country of Yugoslavia, which is now in the process of being bloodily unraveled into its separate nations. In Austria there were uprisings after World War II. The Social Democrats had called for a revolution, but one without violence. They therefore checked a real revolutionary movement. Austrian workers' and peasants' Soviets had sprung up in this country. The revolution was crushed, after fighting in the streets, because those in power were ready to use violence to suppress it, not to support it. The Austrian worker had fought valiantly in the streets of Vienna, against the admonition of the Social Democrats. The great shell holes that my husband and I had see in the Karl Marxhof were witness to the military might used against the workers. At the same time, the Hungarian workers also rose up and formed Soviets. They begged neighboring Austrian Social Democrats to help them with arms, which were refused. In Poland, too, there was an uprising. Europe was a boiling pot.

Harold Laski, M. P., under whom I took some courses in Political Science at the London School of Economics, said that in politics, there is never a choice between black and white, but between different shades of grey. But this was the voice of Social Democrats who had failed dismally in Europe. If all these revolutionary movements after World War I had been successful, the USSR would have been enormously strengthened. Lenin would not have had to make his "two steps forward, one step backwards." The whole face of Europe would have been changed with a conglomeration of socialist states.

In faraway China, there had been uprisings both in 1913 and 1915, which had been beaten down. Lenin was immensely interested in China, where he saw a large peasantry and a small proletariat, who had to be led to fight together as in Russia. Yet he foresaw such a coalition, if under the leadership of Kuomintang would be sold out to the Chinese "Whites," as Kerensky had been attempting to with the Russian "Whites." Writing his last thesis in 1923, he foresaw, too, the revolutionary Chinese movement if it were successful, unleashing a similar movement in India. By 1927, Stalin had taken power, and he in contrast with Lenin, urged the Chinese Communists to join with the Kuomintang, only to have thousands of them slaughtered in Shanghai. It took Mao Tse-Tung a while to rebuild an army and to undertake The Long March and the fight again that would achieve a successful revolution.

World War I had ended in November of 1918. The unrest continued into the twenties, though subdued, it was still there and was beginning to merge again in the early thirties. We young students, who had been children in World War I, had to learn this history before we could begin to understand what was happening in our time and that events now were the result of what had happened previously.

Unfortunately, there was no longer Lenin and Trotsky in Russia to offer the proper advice and help that was needed in this second revolt in Europe. Trotsky was in exile. He offered the right advice, but he no longer had the power to effect events.

Stalin had stolen that power. He had also devised a new theory, "Socialism in a Single Country." He wanted quiet and stability in Europe, so he could deal solely with his domestic problems. Therefore, his foreign policy was inevitably to sabotage the new revolutionary elements surfacing in the late twenties and early thirties.

In Spain, there was the overthrow of the monarch Alfonso XIII, followed by the Civil War, which lasted for six years, from 1931 to

1937. This was going on then for almost the entire time of James's group's existence. In the Spanish Civil War, the Russians were supposed to be helping the anti-Franco forces, and they did to some extent. They provided arms and help but only to those who were following the Stalinist line. The POUM, the Spanish sister party to the British ILP, was denounced and fought. The Communists were destroying and fighting as much against the various anti-Fascist forces that were not aligned with them, as they were fighting the Fascists themselves. The name for all Anarchists, Liberals, Trotskyists, became Social Fascists. Because of this, the failure of the revolution should be planted at the door of Stalin. Of course the failure of the Spanish Civil War would, in its turn, lead to the failure in Germany. The viciousness of Franco would be repeated by the Nazis.

In France, too, there was a prerevolutionary situation beginning in 1934 of which we were witnesses and which also failed. James had been sure of its success. The working class had entered the Communist Party in great numbers, believing in it. They, too, were ready to set up Soviets against the French fascists; they poured into the streets by the thousands. The Communists allowed demonstration after demonstration but held them back from further action because Stalin wanted a Franco-Soviet Pact for the defense of the Soviet Union.

In Italy, after a struggle between the workers and Fascists, Mussolini came to power. Mussolini was an old Socialist. He had promised health and old-age insurance, an eight-hour working day, minimum wage, workers control of factories, high taxes for the rich—in fact, a socialist program. He offered this to the working people, to the middle-class, white-collar working people. He had no intention of carrying out such a program. The socialists of 1921 had a million and a half votes; the Communists about three hundred. The Democrat-Liberals trusted in the King of Italy and the Italian Constitution, and so Mussolini was able to march on Rome and begin his brutal routine. People were quickly disillusioned, especially after the murder of Matteoti, one of the socialist leaders. There were all the signs of rebellion, but Mussolini crushed all opposition.

In Abyssinia, Haile Selassie was facing threats from Italy. The Fascists' ruler, Mussolini, wanted to establish an empire. He had called up his military and had refused all offers of conciliation. In October 1935, the Italian invasion began. In May 1936, Addis Ababa, the main industrial center, was captured. Haile Selassie fled the country, and the King of Italy was made emperor of Ethiopia. Mild sanctions were established by Great Britain and France against

Italy. It was not until after World War II that Great Britain had enough influence to bring back Haile Selassie.

Hitler, in his turn, at first had offered some vague socialist ideas, but they were so flimsy, the big capitalists and the big billionaires were able to give him their support. This included rich men in the United States. Trotsky repeated and repeated his urging that the general mass of workers must unite. He wrote two pamphlets in 1931 and 1932, which all in our group read: *Germany: The Key to the International Situation* and *The Only Road*. Both books called for the workers to unite. He saw the crushing of the workers' movement in Germany as a blow against all the workers in Europe. In the beginning of 1932, in the elections, Hindenburg still had the majority of votes; Hitler could have been prevented from coming to power. it was not until he did, and there was no turning back, that Stalin's forces would change their slogans. Not until the defeat of the German workers, when it was too late, did Stalin call for a United Front; the Stalinists were splitting the working class by calling the socialists, and all who disagreed with them, Social Fascists. The workers had to be united to fight Fascism. Fascism has to be fought and conquered in the countries in which it appears. It cannot be fought by wars. It is the genesis of war.

In Germany, the Stalinists, instead of aiding the socialists in fighting the Fascists in the streets, were fighting the socialists. These were then years when the Far Right in Europe gained ascendency. In 1933, when C. L. R. James formed his small group of intellectuals in London, the dark tide of reaction was midway to its peak: We young idealists to the Left, hoped by our speeches and our writings, directed by Leon Trotsky, to help stem that tide. Of course, we, our tiny group, were not alone. Trotsky had helped form and then direct such small groups throughout Europe, Africa, and also in the United States. We were not alone, too, in that other people in other ways were attempting the same task.

One instrument that should have been there and that could have given enormous strength to this antiwar movement, the Communist parties in the various countries, in the Third International, betrayed their revolutionary role. Stalin's name had been added to that of Mussolini, Hitler, and Franco—all ruthless dictators against the working class.

In England, there had been class struggle evinced by the General Strike and succeeding smaller strikes. The rise also of a Fascist Party led by Oswald Mosley: the economic depression, too. And the overthrow of the current king. I was with James, when Stanley Baldwin, the prime minister, dethroned Edward VIII in 1937, after a 325-day reign. James said; "This will be the beginning of the end of the Royal Family, when one of their members can be ousted by a Prime Minister." In this I think he was prophetic, for the Royal Family has been steadily disintegrating. They have to marry commoners, who have not been brought up from childhood in the traditions of royalty. They are divorced; are subject to rumor and gossip. There soon might come a time when, with this breakdown, people will begin to wonder whether to keep a queen on the throne, the richest woman in the world, and whether those around her, in the royal family, should own so much of Great Britain's wealth, including vast acres of land, many palaces filled with treasures that should belong to all, fabulous jewelry worth a king's ransom. Some Labour M. P.'s are calling for the end of the monarchy now.

Rather than this small group of people owning so much land and treasures, my own view is that if they were given large mansions and estates with an income to match the needs of upkeep, with a large number of horses and dogs, they would all be as happy or happier than they are now. Their tedious duties, trotting around the globe, which drums up trade, I am told, could just as easily and far less expensively be done by experts. The British nation would enjoy a great increase in its wealth. I think, as James did also, that the time is coming.

In the United States, there was the Great Depression whose ripples were felt throughout Europe. The economics of the situation were, as always, at the root of the evil. The wealthy, and therefore, the powerful, wished to become more wealthy and more powerful, which could only be done at the expense of, and deaths among the poorer, the working class. The workers in all countries had to unite if there was to be any victory for their mutual cause of international peace. By this interest only in his own power in his own country, Stalin split the masses in the various countries, and so led inevitably to their defeat and the inevitability of large-scale new war.

Our attention had focused on Abyssinia, Spain, China, France, Italy, Germany, and then, on the Moscow trials. The Labour Party, though not generally left wing in its sentiments, called on Stalin to ask why, if there was democracy and justice in the Soviet Union, Trotsky had been expelled, and why now there was the extermination of thousands upon thousands of old heroes of the revolution. At the public trial of their leaders, plots that were supposed to have taken place at a hotel in Denmark were proved to be false because the hotel had for many years not even existed. There were many such instances that showed how false the evidence was against these old men, now old heroic men. The amazing point was that they should all have confessed. Did they think that this was a last duty to the Soviet Union, a last duty they could pay to try to preserve as patriots their country's honor, right or wrong? Was it that they had been subjected to too much humiliation, too much torture, or that their friends and their families were too endangered if they did not give that final humiliating confession? It was a sad sight throughout the world, not easily forgotten. It, too, was one of the great events of our times.

The Moscow Trials organized by Stalin, were enacted on the world stage during the five years of James's group's existence. The trials lasted over a long period with new victims being brought out, from time to time, to prostrate themselves before the Stalinist dictator. The Communist press, throughout the world, heaped calumny on them, and in many cases, was able to convince public opinion of the likelihood of the crimes that these men were supposed to have made against their own country; of their treasonable behavior. But, on the whole, the intelligentsia of various European countries, and of the United States, did not believe in the mockery of the trials. Only in such purges could Stalin deal with the very slightest dissent in his country. The men in top positions were now his men who carried out his orders without hesitation, without thinking, or perhaps even thinking that their own necks would be in danger if they did not do so. In this way, the great stifling bureaucracy in Russia was built up through the country. Everywhere there have always been bureaucrats ready to take advantage of their positions, but in no case was it so all pervasive as in the Soviet Union. The Soviets actually had been a very democratic form that had risen in the 1905 revolution. Then the men and women, the people, chose within their own small groups a leader. Those leaders then met and within the next layer, they chose the men just above them and they could always replace the men they had chosen. So that when people decry the Soviet system, this is wrong, because it had started out a very democratic form of government. Its roots were firmly placed on a wide base. Trotsky himself had been chosen as the head of the Moscow Soviets during the Revolution of 1905. But the pyramid solidified until the man at the top Stalin became the Great Dictator. In Cuba the pyramid system still exists, but it is fluid, and Castro is a leader and not a dictator.

Trotsky, in his early rejection of Lenin's tight party of selected cadres, saw it rightly as an: "Organization where the Party substitutes itself for the people, the Central Committee substitutes itself for the Organization, and finally, the Dictator substitutes himself for the Central Committee." Rosa Luxemburg agreed. Lenin's tightly centralized party could only lead to the emergence of a dictator, she said. Of course, it did.

One of the great "ifs" of history is how different the Soviet Union might have evolved if Trotsky had succeeded to power against Stalin when Lenin died. Lenin himself, before he died, was stricken by the realization of what was happening to his party, and where the General Secretary of the Party, Stalin, that "peppery cook," was leading his beloved country. In the Soviet Union, the betrayal of the revolution had begun by Stalin while Lenin still lived.

While Lenin lived, Trotsky was the second most brilliant figure in Russia. His organization of the Red Army gave him an international reputation. He was the greatest orator in Europe. He became personally known to and beloved by millions. His pamphlets appealed, as James wrote, equally to professors and peasants. Most important, of all, he was Lenin's right hand and believed by all as his successor.

In the Soviet Union itself, Stalin would take over for himself the Five Year plans of Trotsky and would put them into brutal practice with haste. For him, fast industrialization became an obsession, using Stakhanovite workers that set a pace others could not follow. Collectivization, which should have been introduced gradually, had been enforced immediately. Thousands upon thousands of small farmers were killed or driven to Siberia, since they had now become in a new policy "Kulaks," that is, rich and exploiting farm owners. Both at home and abroad, Stalin's policies were disastrous.

One of the reasons for Stalin's rise had been the result of Lenin's tight party. This was correct when the masses needed direction but should have been loosened once the Bolsheviks achieved victory. Early, there had been those who questioned the wisdom of the tight party and the use of centralized power. One of them had been Plekanhov, who prophesied: "The ultimate end of all this will be that everything will revolve around a single man who, ex-providential, will concentrate all power to himself."

Lenin himself recognized the danger too late. Just before he died, he issued a Testament warning of the perils that a split in the party would bring, because he reminded the Central Committee that the party rested upon two classes, not one: the workers and the peasants. He wrote: "For that reason instability was possible, and if there cannot exist an agreement between the two classes." He prophesied correctly "its fall is inevitable." In his Last Testament, he wrote:

> Comrade Stalin, having become General Secretary, has concentrated an enormous power in his hands; and I am not sure that he always knows how to use that power with sufficient caution. On the other hand, com-

rade Trotsky is distinguished not only by his exceptional ability—personally, he is, to be sure, the most able man in the present Central Committee—but also by his too far-reaching self-confidence and a disposition to be far too much attracted by the purely administrative side of affairs.

These two qualities of the two most able leaders of the present Central Committee might, quite innocently, lead to a split, and if our party does not take measures to prevent it, a split might arise unexpectedly.

December 25th, 1922

POSTSCRIPT: Stalin is too rude, and this fault, entirely supportable in relations among us communists, becomes insupportable in the office of General Secretary. Therefore, I propose to the comrades to find a way to remove Stalin from that position and appoint another man who in all respects differs from Stalin only in superiority—namely, more patient, more loyal, more polite, and more attentive to comrades, less capricious, etc. These circumstances may seem an insignificant trifle, but I think that from the point of view of preventing a split and from the point of view of the relation between Stalin and Trotsky which I discussed above, it is not a trifle, or it is such a trifle as may acquire a decisive significance.

—LENIN

Stalin's first move against Trotsky was not to inform him in time, so that he could be at Lenin's funeral. An ill Trotsky was in the south of the country at the time. But the fact that he was not there caused people to think adversely against him for not attending and paying "his last respects."

Why did he not call a mass meeting, and, superb orator that he was, tell the people how Stalin had not informed him of Lenin's death till it was too late to attend the funeral? Stalin then would have been shown to be the schemer he was. Stalin had, during Lenin's lifetime, filled posts of importance throughout the country with his own men. Trotsky's talents were not those of his wily opponent, and he lost against him. Slowly, he lost power and his following until he was driven finally into exile. From there he took on his adversary with his pen, writing brilliant books on what should be done at home and abroad.

Over the policy in the case of Germany, then paramount, Trotsky had been advocating the policy of uniting all the workers. But Stalin went beyond that and called for a United Front of all classes against Hitler. The cry then became, "After Hitler, Us," as if Hitler's ascendency would be brief and harmless. It seems incredible today that there should have been such a cry.

Realizing his past illusion at last in May 1935, Stalin signed the

Franco-Soviet Pact as a pact of war, a preparation in case of a Hitler attack against Russia. Even in the end, the United Front called for by Communists did not mean workers unity, but meant the unity of anyone who would be against Hitler's war, who would surely turn, at some time, against the Soviet Union despite a last-minute pact of Germany and the USSR.

Since Stalin had come to power and issued the slogan, "Socialism in One Country," it had meant the Soviet Union was turning its back on revolutionary movements around the globe. The Communists parties, in other countries, were only there to support the policies of Stalin, whichever way he turned. Now he tried to get everyone to join together for the support of the Soviet Union and the fight against Hitler's coming war. This meant support of World War II, but on the side of Russia.

Our group of Trotskyists then saw its role as battling the Communists everywhere to overcome their disastrous betrayals. The background of our activities was the great volcanic upheaval beginning to spread its ashes over the whole of Europe. In contrast to Stalin's "Socialism in a Single Country," Lenin had written that the victorious revolution in one country consists, "In the development and support of the awakening of revolution in other countries."

James and the others in the group, believed that in the coming war, as in after World War I, a revolution had broken out in Russia, so uprisings and revolutions would, after World War II, again break out in France, Germany, Austria, Hungary, Italy. We also believed it would happen in Great Britain. We were right that Great Britain in the new war would lose its empire. I look back at our young enthusiasm and optimism for the future and realize that none of the hopes that we had then were fulfilled.

In 1935, James was working on the writing of *World Revolution 1917 to 1936: The Rise and Fall of the Communist International* (London: Secker & Warburg, 1937). These were almost the twenty years since the Russian Revolution and the revolutionary movements that this had touched off in the other countries of Europe. He dealt with the 1789 French Revolution and with Marxism, also with the impossibility of a national Socialism that Stalin was now proposing in the form of "Socialism in One Country." The idea was that Socialism could be worked out in the Soviet Union without regard to workers' movements in other countries, that Communists all over the world should be no more than supporters to what was happening in, Russia. CLR dealt with Leninism: wrote about his Democratic Dictatorship of the Proletariat and Peasantry; as well as Trotsky's thesis of Permanent Revolution. He dealt with subjects from Engels to Reform of the Second International: and the First World War as well as the role of the individual in these events. He included his analysis of the German Revolution and the Austrian revolutions and how these had been crushed and stabbed in the back by the Stalinists. He told of how Trotsky's Five Year plans had been taken over by Stalin and distorted and how wrong was Stalin's attitude to the peasantry, whom he now called Kulaks. He dwelt on the Chinese Revolution, too, and how this had been betrayed by Stalin and how fantastic Stalin's call was of "After Hitler, Us." In fact, he showed how the revolution had been abandoned by Stalin and how now it was necessary to build the new international, the Fourth International called for by Trotsky. It was a massive piece of work and a great deal of research had to be done to complete it. But James did, within a year, though he had members of the group to help him in one way or another in both starting and in finishing this big project. However, with the underlying youthful optimism that pervaded us all at that time, he made many mistakes in his prognosis and prophesies. If he had lived a few more years, he would have seen today the dismemberment of the Soviet Union and its socialist structure and its moving toward a capitalist and market economy.

The rest of us, except for James and Charles, went on plodding and on being good foot soldiers, helping in any manner that we were able. James asked the question: "Why did Stalin persist in this policy, that is in the policy of not believing in the revolutionary potential of workers outside of the Soviet Union?" He asked further; "How could the Soviet bureaucracy possibly conceive that any useful purpose could be served by letting Hitler come to power?" According to James, "No question is more important not only for the past but for the present. In the answer to it lies the whole complex problem of the relationship of the international working class movement and the Soviet bureaucracy. The root of this suicidal policy which has such catastrophic consequences lies in the very nature of the workers' bureaucracy inside as well as outside the Soviet Union. We shall understand the Soviet bureaucracy better by noting how closely it resembles the workers' bureaucracy with which we are more familiar." James pointed out that "The social democracies in the other European countries are far more hostile to their own bourgeoisie, and that the Soviet bureaucracy is also far more murderously against Trotskyists and other revolutionaries in Russia, than it is to the bourgeoisie of France and Britain."

It is from that bureaucracy, built up in the Soviet Union in the fifty years from Stalin onward, that Russia is in such disarray today.

All these various world events would undoubtedly have been changed if Lenin had lived, Trotsky succeeded him, or Stalin had been removed as Lenin had instructed. Stalin, as much as Hitler, was responsible for World War II and its manifold tragedies. Stalin's policies meant, too, the failure of the Third International that Lenin had formed after the Second International had discarded its premises, and the Socialists in all the countries involved had supported the Second World War. So now it was time for the Fourth International that Trotsky initiated. We were internationalists. James went as our group's representative to its inauguration. But alas, I hear no word or it today or even know if it still exists.

All these noted events were the background of international turmoil that we, the small groups of Trotskyists around the world, faced in the thirties and incredibly hoped to defeat. This was the background that we, C. L. R. James's small group, discussed and discussed around the table in the bedsitting room in London in the Thirties. I believe I am the only one now alive who can give a true account of it.

It is sad and may now seem pathetic, that this small group formed by C. L. R. James, sitting around that table in that dusty room could have hoped to have an effect not only in England, but with others, internationally. It was not that we were intellectually arrogant but lost in the excitement and camaraderie of high visions that perhaps only the young can aspire.

But how we talked. How excitedly and seriously we talked, and C. L. R., our leader, the born talker, talked most of all. Yet being in that group, with such a man as James, changed us all. As we would go our separate ways later, still the mark of those days of our youth, when we discussed and discussed among ourselves, myself among the others, my warm hearted comrades, listening with eagerness to C. L. R. James, that mark would never be lost to us in memory: those years when we all had been so pure in heart, wanting to save the whole world from its ills.

4

James and I Go to Paris

ONE DAY, ESTHER HEIGER CAME TO MY HOUSE AND TOLD ME EXcitedly that James was going to France, and she said, "Could not the two of us go with him?" I thought about it for a little while and discussed it with my husband. We decided that I could. James went ahead, and he found us a room with a washbasin and lavatory in Montparnasse where he was staying. Cafes in Montparnasse were favorite meeting grounds for the Trotskyists at that time (as well as the rendezvous for artists and writers), such as in Le Dome and Les Deux Magots in Montmartre. We used to go to those cafes for lunch and dinner. We also used to go out to the markets for fun and to buy oddments, and, of course, we met James every day. One very amusing item. James's French was poor, though he had made two earlier short trips to Paris. However, James could not bear to be silent. It really angered him that he could not fully express his views in French. He became almost fluent in French in three weeks because of his feeling of impotence when he could not talk and argue with people. Of course, there was also his phenomenal memory. He remembered all the books he read; he even remembered page numbers; and often when he was making a speech, he would "slay" a heckler by referring to the page and line of a quotation from a certain book. He was equally sure that the heckler could not respond with such specific detail.

Still Esther and I were not seeing James all the time, since he was visiting other people. I think he went to see Lev Sedov, Trotsky's son, who died soon after their meeting. Previously, James had been to Paris twice. Both were short visits during the time that he was in the north of England as a guest of Learie Constantine. He was working on an outline for his book *The Black Jacobins*. At the time of the Haitian Revolution, Haiti was a French colony. Toussaint L'Ouverture and Desalines had beaten back Napoleon's forces from France sent to put down the revolt in the Caribbean island. James needed to visit the Paris libraries. He could read

French. A visit to Paris seemed needed. But James had no money. A friend of Constantine's, a well-off businessman, staked James's first visit. When he returned, James told the businessman an enthusiastic tale about Paris and in particular about a beautiful woman he had met there, so that the businessman wanted to go to the "city of lights," too.

James and he went again for several days, so that the business man could meet the dazzling Parisienne. What happened between the North of England businessman and the woman is not known. But it is said that all three went out and had a good time together. While there James had made some cursory sightseeing, but there was still much to visit.

I myself had visited Paris earlier once with my family when we were vacationing in France, and later with my husband. However, it was a great delight to see Paris again with James and Esther. We meandered along the Left Bank, turning over and looking at all the books on the stalls. Esther and James went to the top of the Eiffel Tower. I stayed below because I am afraid of heights. With not much enthusiasm, Esther and I accompanied James to the Military Museum.

It was springtime in Paris, the loveliest time of the year, and we sat outside the cafes, drinking wine and trying our first taste of absinthe. We went with some of the French comrades and also one or two of the *Partisan Review* people we met. James, as usual, tried to do most of the talking, with Esther and I being given little opportunity to join in the discussions of the men, though I stoutly intervened now and then. It was an exciting time: always with much more for the three of us to see and enjoy.

Almost daily we made a new excursion, and all the time James talked. I think he was glad to get back to the English language after his strenuous efforts to speak French. The memory of that French vacation stayed with all three of us for a long time. James went alone twice more on political business as a representative of our group to two conferences.

We also did some sightseeing: mostly for Esther, but because these were sights of which it was possible to repeat and repeat with enthusiasm. We went to Le Louvre and together enjoyed seeing the Roman, Greek, and Egyptian antiquities. With pleasure, we looked at the vast collection of art starting with Cardinal Richelieu offerings and going on to all the art that Napoleon had collected during his conquests. Naturally, too, we gazed upon and discussed the collection of French Impressionists in the Jeu des Paumes as we wandered with delight through the Tuileries Gardens. Naturally, we went to see Napoleon's Tomb and the Bastille. We took one day off to see the Versailles that Louis XIV had built, and for us a special site of the French Revolution, since it was never inhabited by a French king after 1789. We wandered about the gardens and park, with Esther chattering and James, always the teacher and the "born talker," giving us several lectures as we wandered from place to place.

Later on, in one of his many letters to his future wife, Constance Webb, he wrote to her that he would love to take her to Paris to see those sights we had enjoyed together. She had heard about Paris only from his letters and never went with him to the French capital. Writing later to Constance Webb when he was in North America, James listed all the places we saw together. He wrote to her: "I would have loved to show you Bastille Square, the Tuileries, the Louvre, the Luxemburg Gate, Champs Elysee, the Arc de Triomphe, Montmartre, Place Blanche, Place de L'Opera. The sense of history in every inch, the wonderful food, the social grace of the French people, their pride in their famous capital, the book shops (they say there are more book shops in Paris than the whole of England), the open book shops on the Seine—a great capital throbbing above and when you look over the bridges on the Seine down below white sand and people—fishing! To say nothing of Versailles, which is the most wonderful place in the whole world I think."

James and I saw all those places together. Meeting with French comrades did not take up all our time. I think he only went back once or twice briefly to Paris. I went back a number of times. But I think we both remembered our time together in that ever enchanting city.

Then he and I went on a separate jaunt together. Excitedly, Esther had told us that one of the French comrades had asked her to go out with him. When she had departed, he turned to me and said: "Why don't we go to *Le Bal Negre?*" He knew that I enjoyed dancing, and so we made this expedition to the night club together. It was not a very fancy place, but it was filled with people. There were blacks of every height, weight, and shades of color from all parts of the world where there are Africans or people of African descent. The women were either the wives of the men, probably some from the diplomatic circles, a good number of French women. I believe I was the only English woman or North American woman there.

We sat at a small table and ordered white wine. We sat for a few minutes until the waiter brought the wine and glasses. James was obviously anxious to dance, and I was ready at all times to dance. It was a pleasure that we seldom had in London. So we danced and danced. James was really only proficient in a fox-trot. I tried to teach him the tango, but he was not very interested in it. So we kept on with the quick fox-trot going back to our table for a rest and drink, but soon going back to the dance floor again. He held me tightly in his arms, and when he took me back to my lodgings outside where the concierge was seated, he held out his two hands to me. I took them and smiled, and he looked into my eyes a long time before he let them go.

One day, James came to us in our lodging and pulled me aside from Esther, and said, "I want you to go out with me this evening." James told me to wear something that was unobtrusive . This was really unnecessary because I always wore rather quiet clothes, fawn, grey, a light blue, a white frock on occasions. When I had worked at Vogue, I had always worn a well-cut, simple black dress.

I had brought few clothes with me to Paris. I selected a grey linen frock with a small white collar and white cuffs on short sleeves, a white belt, black shoes, and a black handbag. And my short hair was covered by one of those silly cloche hats in grey.

It was nearly dark when I met him—*l'heure bleu,* a time of slight *tristesse,* a slight sense of sadness, of foreboding. We met without Esther Heiger, and then there was a good deal of cloak-and-dagger stuff. We would go a little way on the metro, then we would hurriedly change, and then we would change again, and then we would go by bus, and then we would change again. It was all to prevent our being followed. I did not take this too seriously. Finally, we arrived on the outskirts of Paris and went to a rather large glass-enclosed restaurant. We approached a young man sitting alone and pulled up our chairs to his table.

James had been quite serious and had hardly spoken until then. On the other hand, I was a little excited, and felt we were off on a small adventure.

The young man I think was in his thirties, thin, not very tall, dressed in rather clumsy clothing as befitted the restaurant we were in. I realized I looked too prim. I should have dressed more in working-class style. But I had not understood that when James had told me to wear something "unobtrusive."

The young man was highly nervous, his eyes darting to the door of the restaurant and searching around the outside glass windows. He had a cup of coffee in front of him but was not drinking it. James ordered coffee for us, but except for a first sip or two, we also left ours untouched.

My excitement turned to confusion. What was this meeting? James sat unusually quiet.

He was suited much as usual, unnoticeable in a medium-priced, medium-colored suit, white shirt, and darkish tie. He never wore flamboyant colors. They were dull sort of clothes. I had often thought that he must have deliberately changed from the lighter clothes of the tropics to ones reflecting the sober greys of England's rainy climate.

So we three sat somehow expectantly. I did not know expectant of what. The idea of adventure was quickly erased by the tensions of the young man we had joined. When his eyes were not sweeping the room, they alighted on me, examining me closely, as if in those swift glances he could discover all about me, of what caliber I was made.

The young man looked me over and started asking me questions about myself: how long I had been in the movement; my education; my professional experience: Did he think I was disloyal, maybe a spy? James must have already told him this, but he wanted to hear it again from me. At the same time he seemed in a hurry. He kept looking outside the glass partitions and around the restaurant. There were few people in the place and no more had entered since I had made my timid answers.

Then one after the other, both started telling me what they wanted of me. It was a serious proposal, and I sensed the urgency in them. I realized I had to make up my mind hurriedly.

The two men had proceeded to ask me if I would act as Trotsky's secretary and assistant for three months. The need was obviously urgent, so that the questions and reply were repeated. I thought about the proposal; finally said no.

After my decision, Adolf left very quickly, slid away like a shadow. A short time later, James and I left, but went back to Montparnasse this time without any except the necessary changing of lines on the metro.

Obviously, James was disappointed in me. He had felt I would have suitably fit into the role, and that by offering my services, he was being of great help to "the Old Man." He had been sure of me: sure that I was free, was capable; would somehow find enough money to support myself and that my reason for refusing, to go home to look after my husband, was too trivial. But he made no effort to dissuade me.

We learned soon after that Adolf had been found drowned in the river Seine, murdered by the Stalinists. So it is possible I should not be writing today if I had taken that assignment. I also realized that the effort we make to avoid being followed or leading others to Adolf had been a serious necessity.

Working for Trotsky was an opportunity that I missed and that I have regretted most of my life, because it would have been an opportunity to have spent time with one of the great minds of the century: a man whom I greatly admired. It would have been, in some way, similar to what I had found when I had visited and stayed with Bertrand Russell. I would have received a new education. It would have been an enormous intellectual benefit for me to have gone, been helpful, and acted in the needed capacity with Trotsky. But, I was a bourgeois young woman, brought up in a bourgeois fashion, and I felt that I really should not leave my husband for three months. I was duty bound as a wife.

Perhaps if the meeting had been longer, then my response might have been different. However, I made the decision swiftly. If I had had longer to think about it, I probably would still have been torn with indecision. Also, I would have felt a need to consult my husband. If I had said yes I would have needed to be away from England for three months. I doubt if either James or my husband would have had any difficulty in finding a temporary or permanent substitute for me. So the decision might have changed my future relationship to both.

Later, I dearly wished I had made a different choice from the one I made. Yet would there have been a continuing pull between duty, as I saw it, and my intellectual desire? Trotsky would have made an enormous impact on me, surely resulting in change. As it was, it was quickly settled, more or less, before I had time even to realize the proposal that was put before me that evening.

Thinking back over the various moments in life that could have greatly changed its course, this was definitely one in my life. If I had stayed just three months, that would have made a difference. The three months could well have extended to a longer period had Trotsky not been able to get a replacement for me after that time. I might well have become fascinated and devoted to him, so that I stayed on and on. Who knows? But I did not seize the moment.

I am sure if they had given me time to go back to England to discuss the matter with my husband, I would have said yes. But I could not disappear from my husband's life by sending him a note or letting him know or by word of mouth that I was leaving him for three months or longer. My husband I am sure would have agreed that it would have been a wonderful experience for me, a lifetime's opportunity, but I felt I could not abandon him without first discussing it with him, and they wanted me immediately. As a revolutionary I undoubtedly would have gone, but I was still a bourgeois young woman with certain codes of behavior. It was a great pity; a great lost opportunity in my life. Though he regretted my refusal at the time, I am sure it would finally have made no difference to **CLR**.

5

Love Affair

WE HAD BEEN WORKING CLOSELY, JAMES AND I, FOR WELL OVER a year. It is hard for me to pinpoint dates of events that occurred more than sixty years ago. We had obviously been drawing closer and closer to each other. Our viewpoints, and in some ways our development, had been similar. I could not remember ever learning to read. He had been reading the English classics when still a child; so had I. Many of the same books had helped form us mentally. As well as Trotsky's *History of the Russian Revolution,* one of the books in his adult development had been Oswald Spengler's *The Decline of The West* (2 vols. 1926–28).

When I was about twenty, before I married, I had gone alone to Cornwall, to spend part of the summer reading Spengler's classic. It also had made a deep impression on me.

Despite his having been brought up in Trinidad, and I in London, we were both shaped in an English tradition. Though I was never a cricket fan, I grew up in St. John's Wood, where Lord's Cricket Ground is situated. It was natural to go there to see the matches. It was part of the neighborhood tradition. With champagne and strawberries in the summer as part of it.

One day, James told me he had two tickets for a performance of Othello, which Paul Robeson had given him. He asked me to go with him. I told my husband where I was going and with whom. I put on a pretty dress, added a chiffon scarf, a crystal necklace, high-heel shoes and nylons, added a touch of perfume, a touch of pink lipstick (my only makeup then), and I was ready to go.

My husband and I had, by this time, moved from the house in Hampstead Garden City to a flat in Hampstead. I went on a bus, Number 13, to Baker Street, where James was to meet me. From there we went by taxi to the theater.

We had been out together many times to many places, especially our jaunt to Paris, but I sensed this was special. Yet we talked in the taxi only of the work we were doing. We had excellent seats in the stalls of the theater. I knew Shakespeare's plays from reading them at school, acting in them, and seeing them played many times. James, too, was thoroughly versed in Shakespeare's work.

Yet this time brought me a sense of the play's being special. Was it because a handsome black man, for whom I had great affection, sat beside me? Was it because there was a magnificent black man on stage, Paul Robeson, and a white woman, Peggy Ashcroft, Desdemona?

When the lines were said:

> A maiden never bold of spirit
> So still and quiet that her motion
> Blushed at herself. And in spite of nature,
> Of years, of country, everything,
> To fall in love with what she feared to look on.

And replied:

> My heart subdued
> Even to the quality of my lord,
> I saw Othello's visage in his mind.

Could I make to myself a similar response? No, I had always been color blind. One of my closest friends at the university had been a Jamaican. I had mixed with Indian students at the university; been to parties where whites and browns (East Indians) had mixed. There were few blacks then in London.

The performance was excellent: the audience captivated. Thunderous applause. As we were getting up to leave, James said, "Shall we go backstage to see Paul, or shall we go?"

I looked at his dark eyes shining at me, and nodded my head. He guessed the answer. We left the theater, found a taxi, and went to his room. As we walked up the stairs, I could feel his eyes devouring me from behind. I thought: "It was probably inevitable." Yet for a moment I wondered if I should take this next step. It seemed too late then to retreat.

In his room, he put on the light, then crossed over to put coin change into the gas meter. When the gas-fire glow pervaded the room, he crossed back and turned off the light. I had been standing near the door watching him. He untied the blue chiffon scarf, which I had over my hair, then slowly piece by piece, he undressed me until I stood there wearing only my necklace. He stood apart then, just looking at me. My crystal necklace must have glittered in the gas light. Then he came over and laid me down on the bed. Neither of us had spoken a word all this time. He undressed quickly and came over to me. "Desdemona," he said and began slowly caressing me, learning all my body. He was a tender and gentle lover: a wonderful lover, skilled.

When tired, exhausted by delight, I murmured that I must go, we both remembered I had a husband to whom I must return. He said fiercely: "I should have had you as a virgin." We dressed and tiptoed quietly down the stairs, then wandered in the silent streets until we found a taxi. He gave the man money and my address. The driver looked at me curiously. James leaned inside and kissed me quickly on the lips, looking into my eyes and murmuring "Desdemona" again before he shut the cab door.

When I reached home, my husband was waiting for me in his dressing gown. It must have been between two and three in the morning. He said abruptly: "So it has happened." I just nodded. "I have been expecting it," he said, and turned away from me. He could scarcely complain: His adventures had gone beyond the *au pair* girl. I went to the small guest room, and though very tired, I could not sleep, but only reenact happily what had happened to me: my fulfillment as a woman in a stronger manner than I had previously experienced. I had a dark lover.

It was, as he was to say later, two human beings who came together and could not let go of each other. We loved each other very deeply: minds, as well as bodies, attuned. Not his Othello to my Desdemona, but a more equal arrangement. I did not think it could ever end in tragedy. Surely we would not love "not wisely, but too well"?

We lay together mornings, afternoons, evenings. It did not matter as long as we were sure we would not be interrupted. We were always fulfilled. For me, sometimes several times in a short period. He was delighted that he gave me so much pleasure, so much that I sometimes could endure no more of such physical ecstasy. Sometimes, he would let me sleep for a while, and he would get up and start working. Or he would prepare tea and biscuits for me while I slept.

The only disadvantage for me was that I could not properly use the bathroom because it was at the end of a corridor, and someone else might be using it. I always went home as soon as I could after our lovemaking, so that I could be in my modern apartment and bathe and change. Yet it was so little discomfort to endure for our love. We never quarreled, never had any recriminations one against the other. We always were happy together, glad of each other, and the gifts we each brought. He was skilled and practiced, virile, and

I gave myself over to him completely. We made love, and we made love. There was to be no end. Our mutual happiness was complete. We were all the lovers of the classics we had each read. But especially we were together as Othello and Desdemona.

Lying in each other's arms, we would tell of our childhood and youth. James's had been a reasonably happy one, running around with playmates, going with them to the local stream to fish and bathe, in a country where there was always sunshine and warmth. There was a cricket field that he could see from one of the windows of his house. From the time he was small, he would spend hours there watching the game, fascinated by it. From an early age, he and his friends had played the game, too, and soon he would excel in it. On the other hand, I had been a sickly, nervous child, always catching any childhood disease that was going around. I took my religious teaching very seriously. I was a sickly, priggish child, not eager to enter into games. "You look as if you have the worries of the whole world on your shoulders," adults would say. I would answer loftily—"Someone has to."

I worried about the small boys who had to be chimney sweeps, who had to rise at five o'clock in the morning and push their small bodies through the long, black sooty chimneys of rich men's houses, cleaning them, and then little enough to eat. I would read Dickens and grieve over the small children forced to become small thieves and beaten and starved. I hated the winter, because I would get "chilblains" on my hands and feet, so they were perpetually hot and itchy. In my preschool days, I recounted for Nello, I was sent out in the garden daily to play in the snow. The English have a fetish about children being out in the fresh air each day.

"How lovely it must have been for you to go to play in the sunshine always," I told my love. "You have never experienced 'chilblains.'" He would laugh and shake his head, asking me to continue. He wanted to know of the differences between life for children in England and those on his own island. I envisioned him and his small brown companions playing freely in the sunshine. In the winter we had been bundled up, encased in woolly clothes.

He was enchanted by one story I told him. Our house was surrounded mostly by high walls, but on one side, one wall was smaller with railing above it. I was miserably making snowballs and throwing them at the railing when a large fat man appeared on the other side. He was wearing a wide-brimmed black hat, and his long dark coat had a half cloak over it.

He came over near the railing and threw a snowball at me. After a moment of surprise, I grabbed some snow and threw it back at him. We continued this for a short time, and then he left. Neither of us was very skilled, the balls seldom hit their targets. Neither of us had uttered a word in this miniature battle. I began to hope each morning, he would be there, to break the tediousness of my outdoor hours. Sometimes, he would suddenly appear. Then, I would not see him for a couple of days. Later I learned that I had played snowballs with G. K. Chesterton.

"Tell me more about yourself," Nello would say.

"Well, I was very proper, very straight-laced and afraid of God," I would tell him.

"Why and how?" he would ask.

In our house, the lavatory was separate from the bathroom. It was quite large with paneling halfway up the wall and then a green damask wallpaper. The toilet and the tank were encased in mahogany, so that as you entered it looked as if this were a wide bench with an unusually wide back. The seat had a lid that opened and a china pull-handle on the side.

"I always kept my eyes fixed firmly on the ground during my bowel movements," I said.

"But why?" he asked.

"Because God was all-seeing, and he was a man." James laughed uproariously at that little tale.

"So you would have preferred God to be a woman?"

I laughed, too, and shook my head over that little girl I had been.

And the prayers I would say; "If I should die before I wake, then suffer Thee my soul to take."

My family was not particularly religious, but I learned such prayers, so unsuitable for a child; I believe they made me timid and, being imaginative, frightened. I was always afraid of the dark and of unknown black forms that would emerge and envelope me from the large, mahogany clothes closet in my bedroom. While James said his family was fairly religious, religion had not sat heavily on his shoulders. He had a reasonably carefree youth.

When I was young, I was glad that I had a sister. Instead of the loneliness and fear of a single bedroom, I had to share one with my older sister. But still, I was bound by melancholy. My sister would come to bed later than I and find me sitting up and crying, with paper and pencil in my hand.

"What are you grizzling about now," she would ask scornfully.

"I have written such a . . . sad story," I would tell her. I had no literary aims then, only that I knew I could be a writer of stories in which all people would be good and the world a better and happier place.

Nello and I discussed our schooldays. We had both been honor students. While James enjoyed learning both Latin and Greek, I learned only Latin and hated it. These subjects were standard in English-segregated schools. The headmistress taught us Latin. She was an ugly, embittered elderly woman who had warts with hairs growing on her face and hair pulled back in a tight bun. She wore long black dresses with high rigid collars and carried a short wide rod. She never hit us with it, but she often would bang her desk several times, enraged by our stupidity. Naturally, we did not learn. She forced stupidity on us.

One day she had been particularly harsh with one thin, timid girl. The girl went home to lunch because she lived nearby, and so she did not eat with the rest of us in the refectory. On the way home, she was run over by a bus. All of us felt that she had been so bewildered by the headmistress' harassment that she had not looked where she was going as she crossed the road. We were all upset and angry, but what could we do? Before the next Latin lesson began, I the shy and timid girl filled with wrath, took a piece of chalk and wrote in large letters on the blackboard—"Murderess." At that moment, I did not care what happened to me. It was my first stand against authority.

"You see," said Nello. "You were meant to be a revolutionary."

The headmistress entered the classroom, saw what was on the board, erased it, and turned to us without comment but with a grimmer than-ever look. During the Latin hour, she turned and looked at me with a venomous glance. How she had guessed that it was I who had declaimed her, I never knew. I realized she would be my enemy for the rest of my schooldays.

As we lay together, Nello told me how he, too, had suddenly changed from a model student into a wild young adolescent. "My family had such high hopes of me," he said. "And suddenly I stepped out of the role they had set for me. I would not go along the projected path they had mapped out for me—I played hookey. I ran around with a group of boys intent as I was on wild doings, mischief." He thought back. "I even stole small things sometimes just for the heck of it, just for the risk and adventure."

He was never caught by the authorities nor did he ever get in trouble with them. His outbursts were not serious. But the school authorities were upset. So was his father. His father was a schoolmaster, a strict disciplinarian. He would force his son into the path of righteousness. To tame his son, he flogged him. Nello had long marks along his back to testify to those beatings. I would run my fingers gently down them as if I could erase the pain he had suffered long ago in his youth.

I think Nello never forgave his father. For his mother, he had a great affection. She had been an avid reader and would then turn over her books to him. He believed that all the enjoyment he had from reading throughout his lifetime had been a gift from his mother.

"What finally happened to you at school," he asked.

When I was fifteen or sixteen, I had grown much stronger physically, much more healthy, and was ready to challenge the world. Finally, the headmistress had cause to expel me. How she must have gloated over the letter she wrote to my parents asking them to remove me from the school because I was "a disturbing influence."

Almost unknowingly, I had taken an examination that would have given me a scholarship to Cambridge University. I had won. But the headmistress had written to the authorities there that the girl whose marks were almost on a level with mine should receive it instead. How she must have gloated over that too. She had suggested that there were certain elements in my character that would not make me a good candidate. I had never been naughty as the term goes. But I changed from being a religious person to one who questioned God's goodness.

There was all the wretchedness and poverty of the people I had read about in my books. Then there were two tragedies in my family that had immediate impact. First, a younger brilliant brother died of meningitis. He had suffered horribly for six weeks, while my parents could only watch. In those days, there were no sedatives and drugs against pain. So this little boy of eight cried in agony until he died.

Shortly after, another younger brother contacted polio when we were at the seaside on vacation. Again there was little in the way of help that medicine then offered. He was in and out of hospitals. They grafted skin, they tried by primitive methods to lengthen his leg. He was finally forced to wear a build-up boot and a brace.

I did not disbelieve in God, but I felt that if I were in his all powerful position, I would not let people suffer. Gradually, I gathered a group of teenage girls around me in the cloakroom, where there was supposed to be silence, and began querying about how the world was as it was if God was all Goodness. Certainly I, not so good, would arrange for happier life for people.

"So you see you were already a rebel," Nello exulted, as if he had proved right in his choice of me.

"Yes, they said when they expelled me, I would become an agitator," I told him.

"That is why you can speak well to a crowd," he said. "Even though you do not still have confidence in yourself." For him, there was no lack of confidence.

"How did your parents take your expulsion?" James asked.

"Well, my mother was obviously angry and upset, but my father would not let her nor my brothers and sisters bother me about it. When he received the notification, he had snorted angrily, 'Schools!' This was surprising because he was usually such a gentle man. He wasn't angry at me but at the school authorities. "He had hated boarding school and in the end had run away."

"So he was a bit of rebel, too."

"Yes. That was why he would not send any of his children away to boarding school. Only when he died early were my younger brother and sister sent."

"Perhaps," I told Nello, "my own interest in education I took over from him. He also saw that each of us went to a different school, so no teacher could reproach any of us for being less bright than a brother or sister."

James who had been a teacher himself was interested in this. So education was also one of the subjects we discussed.

"But I see you take after your father," he said. "Gentle and rebellious."

Of course, our reminiscences were brought to light over a long period of intimacy.

"Fundamentally, you are like me," he said. "We have so much in common in our characters. That is why we fit so well together." And so we would make love again in the astonished wonder of the pleasure our bodies gave.

Another incident amused James. Our garden, at the back of our house in St. John's Wood, was separated from the one behind by a six-foot wall. In that house lived Guy D'Ardelot, the composer of sentimental ballads for late afternoon and evening soirees such as "Because God Made Thee Mine."

At the time, I was taking piano lessons. What prompted me I do not know, but I would go to the drawing room, open wide the French doors that led to a small balcony, and then on the nearby piano proceed to play the neighbor's ballads. I believe I thought they would be pleased at hearing a neighbor playing their songs. I say they because there was both an elegant young man and an elderly, somewhat fat woman living there. We did not know which was the composer.

They must have found it frightful. Luckily for them, my music master soon after said to me. "Please tell your mother that she is wasting her money and my time by your having lessons." I was thoroughly humiliated. But I did not open the piano again. For many years I had no interest in music.

It was such girlhood incidences over which James and I would rock with laughter. I had not told anyone about them previously, and only in the telling did I realize how funny so many of my stories were.

At meetings of the group, I had usually sat next to James. We often had discussed, between the two of us, subjects that would likely be brought up in the agenda. And then at the meeting, James would put forward the view. At his side, I could pass him notes or prepared material.

However, in the meetings, following our being together, I sat on the other side of the table. I felt that neither of us could withstand the touch of our hands or the incidental brushing against each another. It seemed that the group soon was aware of the situation between us. However, they were decent and discreet about it.

Amongst his intimates, James was called Nello, and occasionally I called him that, but so that I would not make a mistake when I was in a meeting, I called him James, which was after all a first name, and oddly one of my father's. So in front of the group, I continued to call him James.

We rarely used endearments to each other. Occasionally, I might stroke his dark smooth skin and say "darling." Occasionally, he would hold me very tightly and say "dear," but these times were rare. There was nothing to compare with the "honey" and "babe" that American wives and lovers use. Neither, I think, did either of us ever say to each the other, "I love you."

There was one exception to our reticence. A woman friend of mine from the university whom I had brought into the group was extraordinarily angry and kept telling me, "You will regret this, you will regret this. It can come to no good. You should break it off at once." She sounded like my mother, talking to me, scolding me. But I did not really think it was any of her business. Also, I did not think that it warranted the rage she exhibited. I wondered if it was pure concern for me or something more—we had been good friends a long time—undoubtedly, there was concern on her part. In any case, I was happy. I smiled at her and told her that Nello and I loved each other. That was all there was to it. What harm would come, surely only the happiness between us that we were now experiencing.

I spent almost every day with James. We worked: sometimes the group was there, sometimes not. Whatever he was doing, I was there to help him. And then when the day was done, we fell on each other, holding each other close. As he said: "We could not let go of each other."

Much later, years and years later, he expressed the opinion that the physical love was greater on my side then on his, and because of this and because I was a woman who would not accept half measures, we parted. It was not, however, the reason of our parting, and there were no half measures. He expressed himself as delighted with me as I was with him. He always wanted me to spend the night with him, but I was quite silly in feeling that I should go home. I was his lover and my husband knew it, so why should I not spend the night with him? Yet I knew he would be waiting there for my return even if I was returning to my own room and not to my husband's bed. After all, he was now keeping me, and there was a sense of fairness that I should give him this small requirement from me. James told me soon after we had started our affair that he had told Gupta. I suppose I had expected it since Gupta was so close to him—Gupta I am sure, was supplying him with money—and there was really no reason not to tell him.

James said to me: "I told him this was like nothing before; this was very serious." He was holding my hands and looking at me earnestly as he said this. Yes, I thought, yes it is serious, but still there was gaiety in it. We were enjoying being together so much. I know I blossomed as a woman in love blossoms. I know I was fulfilled by him as probably few women are fulfilled by their men. I had a reasonably satisfactory sexual relationship with my husband, but this took me to greater heights. Yet James was always very tender, very gentle. If I could sing, which I cannot, I would think I would have gone about each day, singing. At this time, too, James showed me a letter that he had written to a girl who had been typing his novel for him, *Minty Alley*. They had been having an affair, and he showed me the letter that completely broke it off.

Oddly, I felt a little dismayed, because naively, I had thought that James had been leading a monkish life. I realized it was ridiculous of me, but somehow, that is how I had innocently thought of him. I also did not learn that he was married until that time. I felt rather sad for that half-Chinese woman he had left behind so far away in Trinidad. Somehow I felt I could give him up if she wanted to be with him. Probably she did, and it was solely James who decided that she would not fit into his life.

When James first came to England, he went to the home of the famous cricketer, Learie Constantine, who had sponsored his coming. Constantine was able to arrange for James to become a cricket reporter on the Manchester Guardian. He stayed in Lancashire some months before he arrived in London to form his Trotskyist group.

I was now in the group that James led. I helped in printing our small Trotskyist paper. I had proofread and edited *Minty Alley* for him. I have the copy he gave me inscribed with his autograph saying thanks for the help I had given. I had done research on *The Black Jacobins* for him. In fact, I did much more work for this book, which I found engrossing, than I had for the first novel. Daily, I had attended the rehearsals of his play (based on his book). I was his almost daily companion. Now I was also his love. The remembrance of those times would last as a rooted tree will grow. The air in that room was never fresh. But we were totally unaware of it.

We never talked of our love, rarely used loving words to each other. There was no tinge of sadness as there so often is in love affairs; nor the acknowledgement that as it has a beginning, so it must have an Aristotelian middle and end. We just loved. We dwelt in the present. Tomorrow was far away. We were never 'triste,' always gay with each other. That boyish fellow Nello said he had been came alive again, and I who had never been given to much laughter was full of laughter with him.

There was both pleasure and gaiety between us. We seldom, in fact almost never, had a meal together. He would make tea for me and perhaps have a biscuit for me. The biscuits would be of various sorts from fancy chocolate, vanilla, and pink wafers to arrowroot or assorted ones. As I remember, they were nearly always sweet. It was a teatime meal because the time we had together was mostly at that hour. He liked me to lie naked on his bed while he would usually hurriedly dress. But all the time he would glance at me, puckering his lips, smiling.

"You make me feel as if I'm something to eat," I'd say, smiling too.

And he would laugh at me and mock me and answer. "Well, I find you quite tasty."

I would make to get up, but he would push me back with a pale palm. "Please stay a little while longer, I like to look at you."

If he looked too long, I would stir restively, and we would again take our erotic pleasure in each other. In later years remembering those scenes, I would recall the lives about other past lovers in historical poetry. "Her dry shanks twitched at Paris' mumbled name."

Yet our lovemaking was only part of all we shared together.

Dressed, ready for a meeting or for his speech, passion cooled. We would talk seriously together. Again that talking together was always good: an exchange of ideas; an agreement over an interpretation of a political happening; a recollection of a phrase or thought from our classical reading. We were always in harmony with each other.

It was not just a matter of passion, though it was a passionate love affair. We loved each other beyond our pleasure-giving bodies. We loved the personality of the other. We liked as well as loved each other. We had mutual sympathies. We found we had mutual responses to the outside world. A singing chord in one of us found a singing chord in the other. He said over and over again to me and later was to say many times to others: "We were two human beings made for each other."

There was not a trace of Strindberg's belief in the hostility between a man and woman. We were complementary. Though he hated my having to return to my husband, he accepted it. I saw him go off on various political jaunts with no emotion except the knowledge we would soon be back together. I accepted perhaps better than he did that we could not live together. Later, I believed that it had kept our love woven within the limits of a tapestry, the edges defined. We were both happy during those years we had together.

We did not have meals together except for a quick item on the menu of a Lyons Corner House, hurried suppers when we were going to meetings together, hardly tasting what we ate. They were never gourmet meals. Often I had to produce some cash to pay the bill, but it was of no importance between us. We shared the limited moments we had. Or sometimes exhausted after a meeting, we would find a place for a short rest and a cup of coffee. Other members of the group tended to say good night to us early and leave us alone. We would review the meeting we had attended, its merits and shortcomings, the reaction of the audience. Then we had to go back to our separate homes. But we knew we would meet again the next day. It was a matter-of-fact parting. At times I was vaguely aware that people looked at us a bit askance: a black man and a white woman. But we were not aware of them. They existed almost outside our consciousness. We were never accosted by hostility. If it lurked in the demeanor of other people, our concentration on each other, our intellectual sharing of what interested us, sheltered us from any hostile atmosphere.

At the public meetings at which James spoke, I sat with the audience, listening to well-known arguments and trying to gauge the reaction of the people around me. Because they were, on the whole, special audiences, the response was almost always good and enthusiastic. James was perhaps at his best when he was addressing an audience. He had early found he had this special gift of oratory, and it had developed during the ILP period.

One thing that should be remembered is that James grew up around black people. It was different from that of a black boy in the States. He was part of the majority. He was never belittled by color and grew up without experiencing the racial inferiority that blacks feel in the United States.

I learned from James about his different upbringing. Mine had taken place in one of the great cities of the world; his had been a small town or village on a small island of the Caribbean. My island, soft and green, had an almost permanent drizzle of rain. When the rains came on his island, they came in great downpours. The timid sunshine on my island contrasted with the almost perpetual hot sunshine on his. The flora and landscapes were different. In ours, the trees were dead in the long winter months, with grey and black branches. On his tropical island, there was always a profusion of exotic flowers, great bushes of pink and purple bourgainvilla, and the red tuliplike flowers on the giant flamboyant. And everywhere coconut palms with their swaying fronds at the top of their narrow tall trunks.

I would visualize him and his young friends running around perpetually, as young boys everywhere seem to do, in little clothing, living almost wholly out of doors. they played their games. In his case it was a passion for cricket. It has been told many times how he had a window in the small house where he lived that gave him a perfect view of a cricket field outside where professional cricket was played. But he could as easily have sat in the sunshine on the edge of the field and watched as the other boys did. He grew up then playing cricket as young American boys play basketball or baseball.

Again it has been told many times that his mother was a great reader, and he inherited his book-reading habits from her. But it was from his teachers at Queens College that he must have obtained his love of learning. This was a secondary school to which he had obtained a scholarship, as most of the young students had. It was not a university, but a place where young men from Oxford and Cambridge Universities were among the teachers. They were sent out to the colonies, not only to the Caribbean, but to other lands then under the rule of the British Empire. Choosing to do so, most of them were probably as earnest in their endeavors in education as English Protestant ministers were in their endeavors to teach religion. Their task was to train the brightest boys of the island to take over the lower positions of the administration. They would be a dedicated group steeped in a desire to transfer their own love of learning to these young black boys put in their charge. Their attitude to their students most likely must have been encouraging and friendly. These white men, the only ones with whom James was in contact, were most likely to have been friendly and encouraging and without bigotry.

V. S. Naipual tells a story of a grandfather of Lebrun (James) being a coachman to a white, rich family in one of the other islands. When they went to England, they took him with them. He had to descend the outer stairs down to the kitchen quarters. He was well received by the white servants and always given cake and tea. Somehow, I sense that when I was working with Nello on his book about the Haitian revolution, that I had heard the same story from him. He was writing about a black coachman who had an affection and loyalty to his white mistress.

Our being together in Paris, and enjoying it so much, had brought us ever more closely together. Certainly Esther Heiger had been with us most of the time, but that had not really mattered. We were together, as it were, almost on holiday, although there were many meetings with French Trotskyists on political matters. We had both taken such pleasure in Paris. James was more relaxed than when he was in London. And we had gone dancing that one night. He knew only one type of dance, a fast exhausting fox-trot. However, all that evening he had been holding me close in his arms. I imagine we might have become lovers then if Esther had not been there.

Later, he would tell others that he had first met me at a Socialist dance. There had been one that we both attended, but that had been after the dinner at the Heiger's and after I had joined his group. Perhaps he first became aware of me as a woman that night. But as he was to say: "I was much in demand," we probably only had one dance together. For myself, I liked him, admired him at that point, but did not think of him as a possible lover. Perhaps later he did not want to mention we had been in Paris together.

Francis Bacon said that "Friendship redoubles joys." This was so between Nello and myself. We had both friendship and love.

We passed more than three springs and summers, autumns and winters in his room. In the winter when it was dark by four o'clock, Nello would put coins in the meter of his gas fire. This was our only light. In the summer, the sun shone palely through his dusty windows: on some spring days when there was the ever recurring soft rain, we would find the greyness outside still sufficient for our needs.

The rain streaked thin lines on the dusty panes of glass, but we had sufficient illumination.

We were not conscious of the weather. We saw neither sun nor moon nor stars. The room was a dull setting for our idyll, but we were not aware of it. We had no outward substances of luminous color as Nature gives to lovers in poetry and romances.

It was a workaday book-filled practical room without any ambience of charm. It did not compare with the pleasant flat I shared with my husband. Nello and I found the poetry in each other, and the outer surroundings had no importance.

There was no night or day scent of flowers; no fresh smell of fields, of bluebells between tall trees. No nightingales were heard; no larks. Even the London sparrows and pigeons were all outside, secluded from our view. Ours was no romantic novelist's setting. There were no special sights. We were starkly held by the bond between us. There was no other stimuli than that of our deep feeling for each other, of two naked bodies: my pale self and my dark lover.

6

Consequences

I HAD BEEN HAPPILY GOING ALONG WITH THE PRESENT ARRANGEment without any thoughts at all of the future when James first told me that he had been married in Trinidad to a half-Chinese wife. He spoke of her very tenderly. I asked him why he had not brought her with him. He said this, "She just would not have fitted into my life here."

However, he had been in touch with her. They had been separated a sufficient time, and she was ready to set him free. James said: "I would like to come and discuss the question of our marrying, with your husband." I did not see the reason for this because I could tell him myself. However, James thought he should meet him, man to man.

I told my husband that James wanted to see him and discuss the subject of our getting married and of divorce proceedings. But my husband angrily refused to see him. He said: "If you want to go to him, okay. Go with your head high. But I will not help you to take a step in that direction." He turned away from me, then turned back angrily. He said: "Don't you know I do not want you to go. I love you, I love you probably as much or more than he does." And then he strode from the room.

I reported this to James who was rather disconcerted. I think he had rather looked forward to the drama of the meeting with my husband. He wanted to say to him: "I am taking your wife from you."

Now that the question of our getting married had been brought up, I was awakened from my pleasant dream of our love affair. We loved each other very deeply. But how were we going to manage when we got married? James seemed to feel there was no difficulty in that; I would just move in with him. However, for me this was impossible. I could share the room with him; I could not share the lavatory and the bathroom that he shared with other tenants, many of whom were transients.

I suggested that I could get a job in journalism very easily and that we could have a quite pleasant but modest apartment. For James this was not a solution. He was very stubborn about it. He could not see himself supported by his wife in an outside job. He wanted me, as I had said earlier, as a Krupuskaya to his Lenin, beside him and working with him on all his writings. On my side, the lavatory and bathroom sharing with others was impossible. I could not accept it. Nor could I accept being supported by other people, as he also suggested. Gupta, he said, had enough money. So we were at an impasse.

It might be thought I was being hypercritical about independence, when I was allowing my husband to keep me. One factor was that he did not want me to go. Second, I functioned as a housewife for him. We had a daily maid, and I oversaw what she was doing. Usually, I made the beds and did the shopping. I made the supper if I was going to be home. If my husband was not going out, I would leave a prepared dish for him to heat in the oven. I would still accompany him to visit friends and his parents if he wished and if I was free. I scarcely went to see my own family, and when I did, it was usually alone. No one at my home ever mentioned James.

Many years later, James started writing his autobiography, but he only managed fourteen typed pages. Someone, but not James, sent me a copy anonymously. One incident in it disturbed me very much. It must have been at the time that James and I were lovers because Gupta was the only other actor in it besides James. I do not understand why James could have done so but he asked this of Gupta. James wrote: "There was much discussion amongst some of us of a question which preoccupied many of the young women at the London University." He was totally misinformed on this. There was no such preoccupation; he made it up. He wrote: "This was a question of the superior sexual capacity of black men."

I could very easily have assured him such a question did not preoccupy the students of London University. We had a central building where students from all the colleges met and had dances and where there were editorial offices of our journal. Marjorie Sharpe was the editor then. Later several of her works played on Broadway, New York. I was the theater critic. This question that James raised may have been a question in the minds of his black friends, or just in his. It was not in the minds of London University students. They were all very serious people thinking of their future careers. Then James went on to write that one day to his astonishment Gupta told him that the question had been settled. James said: "I asked him how such a question could be settled." He replied that certain young English women at the university had carried out a scientific but practical experiment on the question. This meant that the young women had sexual relationships both with white students and with black ones. The number of black men were only a scattering, so it meant these young women had to search out the black students at the various colleges and deliberately go to bed with them just to answer a question that Gupta had put to them. It was an outrageous suggestion by Gupta. I am absolutely sure no such scientific experiment was ever done. James then continues that these young women, who had been prepared to make this scientific sexual experiment on Gupta's behalf, said that Africans were more tender and appreciative but about superior sexual capacity, that was fiction. I have never read anything so outrageous in my life and found it extremely distasteful. But I had not heard about this during the time we were lovers.

If James in asking the question was trying to discover where he stood in virility in comparison with white men, I can only say that in regards to myself and my husband, that he certainly was more virile; but this so-called experiment involving some English young women, was completely unfounded and completely untrue. I would say that almost 100 percent of the women at the university were virgins. English women seemed then at that time in the twenties and thirties to develop late. Though we discussed Bertrand Russell's idea of "Companionate Marriage," it was rarely acted on. Most of my women friends married the young men they met at the university.

For some reason James thought Gupta was fascinating to English women. I never found him so nor knew of any of my friends that did. He certainly had no competition with James. When the women fell in love, it was with CLR. Gupta went to the university center often, but I never found any of the women there "falling over" him, as it were. I felt a great distaste in reading this paragraph in James's autobiography and wondered what had led him to put it there.

Did he himself wonder about it? It does not fit into my idea of his confidence in himself. Was he comparing himself with my husband? Why did he put this in his unfinished autobiography?

He never asked me about that side of my relationship with my husband. He may have wondered about it. I had told him about my husband's affairs, but very briefly, in no detail. I would never have discussed with James what happened between us in bed. If he had raised the subject, I would have found it offensive. He must have realized this, for he never did.

Our love affair continued with the question of marriage unresolved. Then a new and dramatic event made us again review the whole situation. I found I was pregnant.

I would have been very happy to have James's child. In fact, I would have been delighted. However, again, there were the practical matters. I saw no possibility of our bringing up a child in his one room. A flat of our own became essential. He then felt that various people would be glad to contribute to our household. For me, I was too independent to accept this. He did not see why other people could not contribute to our support. I knew that I could keep our living together within very modest terms, but I could not take money from other people. I had been a working journalist and could be so again. James felt that his cricket reporting and his books would provide some money. But it would obviously not be sufficient for the three of us. Now, with my pregnancy, it meant that, in any case, I could only work for a certain number of months before I would have to give up whatever job I found. So, even my solution, to a great extent, was invalidated.

We discussed it and we discussed it and we discussed it. He wanted me to marry him and be by his side always. I wanted to marry him and make our relationship permanent. For a long time, I had wanted a child. Now I had the possibility of having his child, I did not wish to forego it. But what were we to do? I was in a state of anguish. Finally, it was decided between us, but woefully by me, that I must have an abortion.

I was somewhat late getting the abortion—I was already two-and-a-half months pregnant—because I had waited a full six weeks to be certain that this was my new condition.

I mentioned earlier that I had a placenta previa, which had caused me a great deal of grief. To save my life, I had to have two transfusions of blood, which my husband had given me. I remember being in the hospital in a general ward. One day, a man came around and he was talking to all the women as he went by, and he came to my beside. He said, "Well Mother, what is the name of the baby to be?" I looked at him in anguish. I could scarcely utter the words, "I don't have a baby, I don't have a baby." He was some sort of registrar of births in the hospital. My breasts were filled with milk, and there was no baby to feed upon me. I cried and cried. They bound up my breasts until the milk finally stopped flowing.

It had been a heart-rending experience. Some six or eight months later, I started having a pain in my groin. At first I paid little attention to it, then it became really bothersome. My husband arranged for me to see a Harley Street gynecologist. Harley Street doctors, as probably everyone knows, are men at the top of their fields, receiving top recompense.

I went to see him in his rather formally furnished office and then went into his examining room. He took some while with the examination, then he told me to get dressed, and I did so. He asked me was there someone in the waiting room to take me home. "No," I said. "My husband is not here. It was just this pain I had been having, and it seemed to be getting worse." The man said: "I hate to tell you this when you have no one with you, but I think that you have a cancer. We shall have to arrange to take you into the hospital, but the hospitals are very full at the moment, and I am tremendously busy."

The pain in my side became worse and worse, in fact, agonizing. The local doctor began to give me morphine for the pain. I can still remember, over all these years, how good that morphine was. How it released me from pain and how it gave me a sort of happiness. But I was waiting and waiting and waiting, and a full two months went by. The pain was getting increasingly worse. Finally, I was admitted to the hospital. Then I went into surgery. And sometime after surgery, probably the next day or later in the day when I had recovered from the anesthetic, the doctor came and told me that I had not had cancer but a baby growing in the left ectopic tube.

So I had lost one baby that I dearly wanted. It was a little girl; we were going to call her Ursula, after one of the heroines in D. H. Lawrence's *Women in Love*. Then I had the second that went wrong and that happens only in one in one hundred thousand pregnancies.

For me then, having a baby had become important. I wanted to have this baby of James. His attitude was not one of delight. I think he felt in some way that a child would not fit into his lifestyle, in the same way as his Trinidadian wife would not fit into his present goals. It was not that he was hardhearted; it merely meant he had set his mind on a certain path of which he was sure he was giving wholly of himself and that he should not let anything obstruct. He was dedicating that life to a cause; and lesser things or even people that did not fit into his main plan were, therefore, to be regretfully discarded. We discussed again the question of marriage. I could only have the child if we were married really, or even without a piece of paper, at least with a home where I could raise the baby. He seemed quite ready if I would take full responsibility for it if I wanted to have it. But how was I to have it? James came up with a solution again. Gupta would help. I could not live on Gupta's charity or anyone else's charity.

I was too independent, so that the decision for an abortion came after a long time of agonizing questioning and despair for me.

Again Gupta was brought into the affair to solve the problem. After some days he came back to James and told him he had been able to make arrangements. James told me and gave me the address of the doctor, and the day I should go there. I hated going. I wanted this baby. Yet, everything conspired against me, so I could not have it. I was desolate.

I could not bring up a baby in James's room; that would have been impossible. And if we were to get an apartment, the question of money arose. I could possibly have gone to my family, but I discarded the idea at once. If they disapproved of my love affair, how much more would they disapprove of my having his child. They would have been shocked even further. The other alternative was to get money from friends. This again, I was too independent to do, so I went to a back street in one of the less desirable areas of London. Trembling, holding myself together by willpower, trying to keep that English stiff upper lip to keep from weeping; this was a desperate back-alley affair. The man was supposed to be a doctor. He had credentials in his one-room office but evidently made his living by doing abortions. I think he had possibly been a doctor but had been disbarred. I got home in a taxi and soon started hemorrhaging. Luckily, I had the guest room, and I tried, as far as possible, to stem the tide of blood myself. I thought I probably should have had medical attention, but as it was, I managed at first on my own.

When my husband came home and did not find me in the living room, he poked his head around to the guest room. I was covered up to my head in bedclothes and told him, "Look I am not feeling well. I do not want anything." He hesitated and I said, "Well bring me a glass of milk and biscuits." I thought if he did that, he would be satisfied. S he came in with a small tray and left it beside me. He said as he was going out of the door, "I will look in later."

However, I think he had an inclination of what was happening. It was very difficult to arrange for all the bloody towels and all the bloody sheets to be secretly washed and to hide my condition from him. We had now an old housekeeper who came in three or four times a week. As she did the laundry, she was horrified at the sheets, and I said she should put them in the garbage. It was impossible to take them to the local laundromat. She got some big bags and with great disapproval, put them in those bags and saw that they were taken away in the trash.

In the end, it was necessary to call our local doctor. He knew what had happened but did not report it as he was supposed to do.

Over some days and nights I hovered between life and death. Nello was upset that I had gone through such suffering and was frustrated that he could not visit me. My university woman friend acted as a communication conduit, not only then, but on many later occasions.

When I next saw him, James said in real agony:

"If I knew you were to be so hurt, I would have drowned myself in Regents Park Lake if it would have saved you."

Yet for his part, I thought he could have taken extra precautions. I had taken those that were then available to me.

My husband, all this time had been very kind. Because of the doctor, he knew what had happened. He was very kind to me during this period. Since I have been with James, I had no idea whether or not my husband had been having his minor flings, and, of course, I had not cared. It no longer had importance for me. I now realize that his forbearance was very great. He really looked after me until I was well again. I believe he felt that this would be the end of my relationship with CLR, that we would resume our marriage, and that he would be a model husband.

My woman friend became almost frenzied when she found out what was happening. She said: "I told you so, I told you so. I knew you should not have gotten yourself into this. I knew it would happen, that you would get hurt. You should never have started it, and thank goodness you have finished with it, even though you have had this sordid business to go through."

I let her carry on and on, but I was too weak and too dispirited to argue with her.

After I was well again, I went back to the group and started working once more. James and I did not immediately resume our relationship. I think he felt very uncertain of me, of my attitude to him: how it would now be.

But we had been passionate lovers, so we could not stay apart. Slowly, but with less frequency at first, we again became lovers. That urgent need was still there, burning in us both. There was no reason that it should have lapsed for James. There was for me, but he still held me enthralled. So again our love affair continued.

When my woman friend realized that I had renewed my love, she was almost speechless. She could not find words enough for my stupidity, my recklessness, my lack of sense. She had told me no good would come from it. As far as she thought, there could only be a repetition of the agony. For me, I went back to the old happiness with James. Perhaps we did not scale the same heights. The abortion had affected me deeply. I was having bad nightmares.

Though I had become physically well, I started to have these very bad dreams: nightmares in which I would wander through dark corridors with lots of doors, and I would try to open them to seek the baby I had lost.

These nightmares were devastating, and they continued for some time. I should have ended the affair with James, but I could not resist his appeal. For him, too, I am sure our love affair went very deeply. The circumstances, however, were against us.

Only when I was in his arms did the shadows disappear.

So the months went by, and I became well again, and I was lying again with him. We fell into the old routine.

We worked together, and at the end of working, we bedded together. Life for us continued in this way for some time. Our lovemaking was still important to both of us. It meant we had this hunger for each other and neither of us had the will to deny it. We clung to each other, but he did not use a foolproof method against conception, though I used a diaphragm.

I think my husband was so upset and disconcerted by my going back to James when he hoped to renew our marriage that he started a new affair of his own. He was frustrated.

So James and I went on with our love affair, while with the group we tried to solve the world's problems. Trotsky still wrote to us. The group in the United States had offered to pay all expenses if James would go there for a period. He was not ready to do so immediately because he was finishing up *World Revolution,* but it was a proposal to which he could look forward. He suggested again that we might go together, but I told him the people in the States had offered to pay all his expenses; we could not ask them to double the fund. Again, what would we do when we went there? He told me they would look after us both. I shook my head. I did think while they would be very glad to have James—they wanted him to go on a speaking tour through the south—I am sure they did not in any way envisage his taking a companion.

Another thought had to enter into our minds in 1937. We knew that the war was coming, the likelihood of peace was disappearing. There was a cartoonist in England called Low, who was very well known. He had a famous cartoon of a cliff in which lots of sheep rush willy-nilly toward its edge and fall to their doom. This was the general feeling in England at the time. It seemed, however, even though we were not sheep, we could not escape from the fate that awaited us over the cliffs. There was no revolutionary spirit to say this must stop. People agonized, but there seemed no way out.

So with James and myself there was the question, with the abortion over, what our future would be. If we stayed in England, James would have been sent to jail as an antimilitarist, as Bertrand Russell had been in the First World War. I, too, would have likely shared his fate.

For me, there is no point in the martyrdom of prison. I have a claustrophobic fear of being shut in, and my spirit would have been broken within a very short time in a prison. With the invitation from the group in the States, James had a way out. While he had suggested that I could go with him, there was no way to believe they had enough money to support us both, or would have wanted to do so. Therefore, he had an escape route from the war and from the dilemma of our marrying. I did not.

Then I became pregnant again: it seemed incredible. I must have been a very fertile woman—my mother had eight children. If I had been living a family life I would probably have had a dozen children, which I would have loved to do instead of later having only one son. Once I realized I was pregnant, I had the second abortion very quickly, in less than six weeks. Someone had recommended a doctor of integrity, who obviously took better care of his patients and did not perform abortions as a general practice, but only on a few occasions. I think someone, possibly Charles Sumner, had pressured him to do so, as a favor. It was done very quickly; this time I gritted my teeth and, in fact, looked on it as having my tooth out. I had no aftermath of hemorrhaging. The whole affair had been swift and smooth.

Somehow I had felt that having only one ovary lessened the changes of my becoming pregnant. However, I was obviously very wrong.

I must have been a very fertile woman to have become pregnant a second time in so short a while. We had used contraceptives, but in those days, they were not 100 percent effective, as they usually are today. It was always hit-and-miss. All my women friends, at the time, were always in a tizzy when their "periods" were due. They were career women, and they wanted to have children later. They were not ready for a domestic life because they were just starting their careers. I think having babies was one of the major topics among us. I know one young woman who, each time she found a job on a magazine, became pregnant. She was full of anger about it. It did not mean that when the baby came she was not a good mother. Unlike myself, she was at least able to keep her children. No "pill" existed.

I had a little money of my own, saved from my days of journalism, from which I was able to pay for both abortions. Nello could not pay for them. I could not ask my husband for the money. I would not let Gupta pay for them.

However, this did mean an end to my affair with James. I had to be the one to walk away. James would not have ended it. It was no longer possible for me to go on. Even I realized that. We had after all "loved not wisely but too well." James accepted my decision with considerable regret. He was to tell the woman who was to be his future wife, he was sad over the loss of me for a full year. This was in 1941, more than three years since we had parted. At the end of 1938, he had made arrangements to go to the States, so that he had a new life in a new country to which to look forward. I went back home to my husband. I told him it was up to him whether he wanted to continue with our marriage. If not, I would give him a divorce, which he could get. But because the divorce laws in England are strict and a divorcing is not so easy, we would separate if he wished. We lived in a period of hiatus for a matter of two or three weeks. He used the time to break off with a young woman he had been going with, to make the adjustments within himself, and then he suggested that we go to Switzerland for a vacation.

For me, I had lost my love. I knew I had to turn my back on James, I had to be prepared to act as well as possible toward my husband, who had shown incredible tolerance. I could not, however, wipe James from my thoughts. It must have been nearly three years that we were lovers. It had been a long time, and we had been very close with a deep mutual love and a fine intellectual relationship. Finally, however, I went off with my husband to Switzerland for a vacation, a lovely healing vacation of mountains, snow, and sunshine.

At first, we slept in separate beds in the hotels in which we stayed, but that lasted only a few nights. He wanted to come to me and did so. As I said, I must have been a very fertile woman because, incredibly, I got pregnant again. Neither of us had taken precautions against it. This time, I could have the baby, and I cannot express the joy I felt. It had nearly become an obsession with me now. The men no longer mattered so much. It was the child on whom I focused my future, all my love, and all my thoughts of delight in having one. The baby would be my life—my lifelong love—though a different love.

James told a biographer that he had spent a very sad year in London after losing me. Actually, we did not break completely. I went to see him often and also continued working with the group, even while I was pregnant.

For James, a new life, without me, was now possible. We did, however, see each other almost to the time of his parting. Then I remember his saying to me after my son was born: "Your son, I will be his godfather. You will see that I am his godfather. If in the future he ever needs any help at all in life, you will send him to me and I will look after him." I thought this was somewhat visionary, but Nello was very vehement about it. But my son never knew that he had a godfather.

At this time, too, there started to be a slight divergence in attitudes about Trotsky. I remained a faithful supporter, but James was already moving away from Trotsky's philosophies, finding fault, even though he was going to the Trotskyist group in the States. These differences of opinion widened while he was there. We did not actually quarrel, but it was the first time we were not in complete harmony with each other. He felt this was the result of what had happened between us. He felt that because we could not get married, I was taking these attitudes that did not fit into his own growing anti-Trotskyism. I knew it was not so and that it was just his masculine vanity asserting itself. He was a very proud, and in some ways, a very arrogant man. You had to agree with him on what he thought. We had previously always agreed.

Later he would break away and form a new group of people who would follow him completely. This is why I think in the very beginning he had to form his own Marxist group, because he could never be just a follower. He had to be the leader. I gathered that through the rest of his life he was, but it was, as I understood it, only by moving from one new group of disciples to another new coterie.

I missed him, but I had my new baby and for me this was an ever-continuing delight. The past, those good and bad experiences were all over. I welcomed and loved the new child wholeheartedly. Thoughts of James became blurred and bearable.

Some time later, the daughter of Sir Stafford Cripps married an African leader and went to Africa with him. The couple had a grand wedding with friends of both the bride and groom attending. The ceremony was held in St. Marylebone Church, our family's church, where my parents had been married; where I had been christened and had attended, in my early years, the church school; where my brothers had been choirboys and my sister had been married.

I was interested because someone with my name had married a black leader from Africa, as I might have married a black leader from the West Indies if he had chosen a different path. Their marriage made me realize it could well have happened that way with me. But I was only aware of the different path many years later, when I was older and politically wiser. We might have found a solution by our going to Trinidad. We never thought of it.

7
New York

So James went to the States to join the Socialist Workers' Party. Barbara and I went into the Labor Party. My husband and I and the rest of England now realized the shadow of war was on us. My brother and I performed in an antiwar play coached by Miles Maleson.

The government was giving out gas masks at local stations, and my husband and I were fitted. We asked about babies, and they told us so far they had no masks for babies. It was now 1939. My baby was a year old. My husband and I had to consider the coming war seriously. We were shocked that they had no masks for small babies. We decided that we should move out of London, though within commuting distance. We chose Welwyn Garden City as our home. Several BBC personnel were moving there. It was a model city, small, well-planned, with a great deal of greenery and the country within a fifteen-minute ride outside the town. Yet the town itself offered cultural events, and the train service was good. When we moved into our new house, we wondered what we should do with my revolutionary library that had grown exceedingly large and decided that we should not have it around if the Germans invaded. There was a small trap-door to the roof, and my husband carried all the books upstairs; they must have half filled the attic. He then made special wooden bars against the trapdoor to hide it and prevent easy access.

Europe was carved up by the Allies after World War I. The victors of World War II would carve it up again. The marching of Mussolini on Rome, the war in Ethiopia, the Civil War in Spain, the Reichstag Fire—the symbol of Hitler's ascendency, his assault on the surrounding countries and Stalin's ousting of Trotsky, the extermination of his adversaries, and the killing of millions in the Soviet Union, had all been preparations for this new war. I wanted no part of it.

My husband's original job at the BBC was with their periodical,

The Listener. Then he decided to become a photographer. He bought up large quantities of photographic equipment and material, and was soon producing excellent pictures. He suggested to his superiors that he go to the States to take pictures of prominent people and pictures showing how that enormous country differed from our small British Isles. An agreement was made. We obtained all our necessary visas and booked passage on the ship, Elizabeth I, to sail on 13 September 1939.

The war broke out September 3rd. No able-bodied men were allowed to leave the country. My husband had to stay in England. Our escape had been planned ten days too late. During this time, Hess flew from Germany to Scotland, and obviously, he carried papers with him suggesting that Hitler would make peace with England. It seemed such an obvious move. When captured, he was first interned in the Tower of London, where past kings and queens of England had been incarcerated. There was mystery about it. Later, when Hess was kept in European prisons his entire life, allowed only minutes to see his mother and son, it became apparent that he had been kept there for political reasons. He was never allowed any freedom. He had done little except make that flight to Scotland. Therefore, why was he in prison all his life? It is hard not to believe that he brought an offer of peace. The right wing of the Conservative Party of England obviously was ready to make peace with the Germans. They felt that England and France should stay on the sidelines while Germany marched against the Soviet Union. In this way when the battle ended, England and France could go and do a "mopping up" operation without having to expose themselves to all the perils of war. This was indicated in the articles in the *Sunday Observer* as late as August 1939, and it was stupidly turned down. Here the extreme right and the extreme left met, except the left wanted no war at all.

Obviously, Stalin was afraid of such a pact, and he made his own pact with Hitler. But this was short-lived. It was indeed apparent that Hitler had no intention of keeping it. The pact gave Stalin a short time to organize his army. He had exterminated many of his best military men. He now needed quickly to recruit new men. It was certain that Germany would go to war against the Soviet Union. Meanwhile, why did Hitler stop when he arrived at the English Channel? It is one of the unknown mysteries of history. England was not ready at that time; Hitler could have had his victory. Perhaps the historians will find out sometime why he made what seems to have been a very foolish move. In Welwyn Gardens City, they made barricades against any Germans marching through the streets, but the barricades were so flimsy that anybody could knock them down with their feet.

My husband continued to work at the BBC, and he was not asked, at that time, to join the army. We began then the nine months of what was known as the "phoney war," with nothing happening. There was an occasional bomber over England, not really many, but the whole country was scared. Rumors of invasions and of men dropping from parachutes filled the newspapers. A neighbor and I supplied a joint air-raid shelter that we had built.

With Hitler at the Channel, invasion seemed imminent. My older brother called me from London. He had been rescued in the Dunkirk operation from the shores of France. He urged me to get to the States with my baby as he had urged his wife. However, she elected to go to Cornwall with her children.

There was an offer from the United States to give homes to women and their children. A ship was going to sail in June 1940, for the States. Since I already had my visas ready when we were leaving on the 13th, it was decided that I should go with our young son. My husband, as a Jew, felt that once the Germans landed he could skip cross-country, which he could do alone, but not if he was burdened with a wife and child. Then he would get to Wales, and from Wales get over to Ireland and find a ship to sail to the States.

I sailed for North America in June 1940. On board were not only British women with their children, but also many refugees from Europe. As the ship pulled out of the harbor at Liverpool, the passengers stood on the decks and cried. None of us knew when we would next see our homeland or what the future might bring. We did not know if we would ever arrive safely at the other side of the ocean. The ship journeyed far north among icebergs to escape from German submarine pursuit. The ship was crowded with sad people.

On the way over, the captain called a meeting and told us of the surrender of France to the Germans. The news was met with further indications of depression by all the passengers. The ship was British, and someone among the British passengers started to sing "Rule Britannia." But the European refugees just crept away.

Searching the ship for a place to escape the crowding, I found one area roped off from the rest on one of the upper decks. I took my son there, glad to be alone. He was managing to walk with the aid of a toy dog-on-wheels that had a handlebar onto which he could hold. I marveled that we could have this solitude. On the second day, however, three women appeared walking along this special area of the deck. When they saw us, one of the women moved to approach me, but she was stopped by the woman in the middle.

The next day, someone told me that we had the Duke and Duchess of Athlone on board. He was going to Canada to take up the position of governor general. The Duchess was pointed out to me by someone else. She had been the middle woman in the three I had seen on the upper deck. The two women on either side of her were obviously her attendants. Alas, I realized I could no longer go to a space reserved for her.

After long dark nights and gloomy days among icebergs, we arrived at Halifax for a short stop. Finally, we journeyed down the coast to New York City.

I had an offer to go to Yale University. Later on I realized I should have taken it, but my independent spirit prevailed. I knew I could work and get a job. I did not want to have to ask someone for haircut money or have anyone be in charge of how my child should be brought up. I realized later that this was not only stupid because I could have gotten a job in New Haven, and I would have been sponsored by the university. There would have been no difficulty. So I could have lived there and been more or less, in an academic circle. It would have been much more pleasant, easier on the child and myself. Possibly at the back of my mind, was the thought that James was in New York. However, I do think it was my desire for independence that was the major factor in my decision.

Soon after I arrived in New York, I was able to find a baby-sitter for a few hours and I took a cab and went up to Harlem. The taxicab driver, when I gave him the address, said, "Ma'am, you don't want to go there. You got the wrong address." I assured him it was not. From James' letters I had his address. So I went, and James was as previously living in a rooming house in one room. He rushed towards me. We fell against each other. The strong ties between us had only lain buried and we made love almost immediately. I heard very little of what he was doing or of what was happening with him in the New York group.

I made a second visit too. Again he made the same proposition to me that he had made in London; that I would stay with him and that the American group would support us both. "As my wife, they would have to do so," he said.

I reminded him that I now had a child. He said: "Well, I think that could be taken care of too." But my child now was the center of my life. I was not going to sacrifice him to any politics. I knew in that milieu, my little boy would be left on the fringe as far as care. I knew that it was stupid to start again with a love affair with James. Again I had to do the walking away. He wanted me to stay, especially now I had no husband in the way. For the second time we said good-bye. In any case it was extremely difficult for me to take time off. I had got a job with a wage of forty dollars a week. Out of this then I was paying forty dollars a month for my rent, and then eighteen dollars for a girl to look after my child in the afternoons. So, that it left me with very little money for our food, or any clothing we might want. The apartment on 82nd Street, was between Madison and Fifth Avenue, a walkup of four flights, an old brownstone, obviously at one time owned by one family. It was up on the top floor. We did have two windows that looked out onto the street which made it pleasant for my little boy who, by leaning on a chair, could look down and see the people and the traffic below the apartment. It had two rooms, a tiny kitchen and a bathroom which had been built in closets, and in which the appliances were ancient. I lived there for six years showing that I could live in somewhat deprived circumstances, if need be. We lived frugally. I remember one Christmas Day we had scrambled eggs for dinner and to my son I gave a few "five-and-ten" toys from Woolworth as Christmas presents.

I had by then found a nursery school nearby, which gave my son, as a British refugee child, a scholarship. It was a progressive school of about fifty children, with John Dewey on the Board of Directors, Dr. Benjamin Spock, not then famous, as the school doctor and later doctor of my son, and Tom Dewey, presidential hopeful, had two children in the school.

It was of course impossible for James to come down and see me when I had a child there. James and I could not be together as lovers. I would not, nor did I have, the opportunity to see him again in Harlem. I only saw him once again while living in New York City. By then, I had been working for some time, and one day, when I was in my office talking to a client, Nello put his head around the door. I made a signal that he should wait, and I tried to hurry off the man with whom I was dealing, but when I had finished, Nello had vanished.

I was not to see him again but once more in the States. Over the years, we did exchange both books and letters. And yes, it hurt seeing him and saying good-bye to him a second time. James had urged me to go back to see him. But soon I realized there was another block against it—racism. When we were in London, the question of black and white never arose. As Nello was to say about our relationship when he was in his "eighties," we were two human beings who came together and then could not let go. When I went to see him in Harlem, the deep attraction was still there. We hardly spoke before we fell in bed. I had paid a second and last visit, knowing I should not go any more.

He brought up the subject then of our being together again. "How could we manage," I asked him. His reply was the same as in London. "The group would look after us. You would be my wife," he repeated as earlier. "They could not refuse."

"And my son?"

He said: "Oh, I am sure they would look after him too."

I had gone through a great deal of travail to have this child. I could not sacrifice him to Nello or to a political group. Their care of him would be casual at best. I still could not let the welfare of myself and my child be at the charity of others.

As I left James a second time in Harlem, I knew that I must never again meet him in a situation where our deep attraction for each other would overcome my common sense. We had finished in London. We must not begin again in New York. I made the decision. In New York, I began to see, as I said, an even more formidable obstacle. If I lived with James, I would have to live with him in Harlem. In London, there had been no such ghetto.

My child, my little white boy, would be brought up in the mean streets among other little boys, all black. How would he fare? How could be fare? I wanted for him the very best that life could offer. I do not mean by this the best that money could buy, though I was not so stupid as to believe that money could not buy many pleasant things. I wanted my son to grow up in an environment in which his mind could develop to its fullest extent. I wanted his talents, whatever they might turn out to be, given the soil in which they could best develop.

I wanted my love to envelop him so that he could grow up free from harm, physically and mentally, and above all, free as far as possible from the many fears that beset childhood. On hearing a police car siren or a fire engine alarm, my small son would immediately dive under a bed or table. So are children less than two years old psychologically hurt by wars: as well, of course, there are those children physically damaged and killed by war. My son would cry "bommer, bommer," one of his first words.

I published a book for parents in that first year in New York, that Jan Struthers of Mrs. Miniver fame, wrote a blurb. She said: "Here at last is a guide to babies which is amusing without being flippant, serious without being stodgy, and deeply touching without being sentimental."

I wrote: "What ever the shape of the world to come, by giving your best to your baby—not material things alone, but your love, your sympathy, your intelligence—you will have equipped him with the inestimable blessings of good health, confidence, kindliness and courage with which to face life."

This was my credo in relation to my child and all children.

Many years later, I got to know Piri Thomas, and he gave me "as a sister" (he had become a Muslim) his book *Down Those Mean Streets*. It shows the despair and hopelessness to which I would have subjected my son if I had succumbed again to my love for James.

How could James stand Harlem? After all he had been brought up on a black island where there was little or no discrimination. True there was the colonial government but his official personal contacts were only probably with his teachers from Oxford and Cambridge. I am sure these would not have given him any sense of discrimination. In fact they seemed to have engendered in him an ideal of the values that were held in England.

When he was in England, he might have found some discrimination but at that time, before the large immigrations from the colonies, there had been little racism. True there were individuals here and there, or even groups of individuals here and there, who were bigoted. However on the whole, he could not have found himself in a Harlem-like situation and certainly he never would have let himself be considered in any way inferior to whites. Quite the contrary he was always a proud, a rather arrogant man. He lived amongst white people, all the time. Our Group was white except for Gupta, and Roy, Indians. He did make contact with his various black friends from different parts of the world while he was in England and met them. But from the time he came to London and then went to Nelson where he was very well-treated and back again to London, he could not have had any sense of the racism that he would encounter in the United States.

I wondered why the members of the Socialist Workers' Party had not found him lodgings either within their own houses or within their sympathizers' houses. Why did he have to live in Harlem? Harlem was a ghetto and he was suddenly thrust into a ghetto. He now could see what racism meant but he never before had experienced it. My two meetings with him were too short for us to go into the question. In fact at that time, it was not a query that was raised in my mind. Later on, however, I began to wonder how he was reacting to it— what his response was. It is curious that he never wrote of his experiences of Harlem or described Harlem from this viewpoint, at any time. I do not know how long he lived in Harlem. I did not know when he married Constance Webb and where they lived. I learnt later that it was in the Bronx.

Here it was in the 40's and a mixed marriage was looked on very unfavorably by most of the population, yet I could not think of her sharing his room with him in Harlem. This is a fact of his life that I do not know has ever been recounted or recorded, certainly not by him. Yet surely it must have had a great effect on him? This is why I find it difficult to understand how he continued to come back to the United States. Naturally when he became a professor at Howard University and the Federal City University, which were both black universities, or when he traveled to give lectures, he would have been well protected. Nevertheless, he had gone down South to talk to cotton growers in his first months in America. From the very beginning there he would have seen discrimination, there would have been at that time, school segregation, bus segregation, segregation in the restaurants and hotels. Presumably he was put up by members of the group who had arranged the tour. But still, he must have seen this glaring discrimination of what Harlem was. I cannot find anywhere in his writings, how he reacted to this particular disgraceful racism in the United States. He wrote on black questions, independence for the Caribbean and for the freedom from colonialism in Africa. But on this point, as far as I know, he kept silent. I am intrigued though, why he would have done so.

On his 70th birthday in London in January 1971, James spoke to a black and white audience. "Now in regard to black people in the United States," he declared, "mentally and spiritually—they have left the ghetto, because you cannot leave the ghetto unless you have somewhere else to go. They are out of it and they are going to remain out of it. Some people talk about genocide. How can you have genocide against thirty million people, or any substantial amount of them? In my opinion, the American establishment is in a lot of trouble with black people. That is their problem, not mine."

Where is the anger in him at what his people in the United States are suffering in ghettos? I feel that anger. How could he have been so seemingly detached? Blacks and Puerto Ricans have to be *physically* out of the ghettos.

When I had gone up to see him in Harlem I had just given the taxi driver the address, we arrived at the door and I ran up the stairs and James was waiting at the top. I, so full of seeing or going to see him, did not really notice the surroundings. It was not until much later that I became aware of what Harlem was—East Harlem for the Puerto Ricans and West Harlem for the blacks. After his initial stay in Harlem, James lived for a further period in New York City for five years from 1942 to 1949. Not Harlem again but the Bronx of blacks, Puerto Ricans, and some whites.

My only journey into the South was not until 1946, which meant that I had not been fully aware of the Negro situation in the United States or at least I had not met it face on. But I went down to Memphis to get a quick divorce. This was done in a weekend, and so long as there was no opposition to it, it went through very simply. I went to Memphis itself, and then the next day had to cross the bridge into Arkansas where the judge gave me the divorce.

However, the one evening when I had been wandering around outside the hotel to look at the streets, I saw an ice cream parlor. Since ice cream is one of my weaknesses I decided I would go in and have some. I saw that there was a notice above one door that said, "Whites" and then the other "Colored." I really was so profoundly ignorant that I thought that they were meaning vanilla or on the other hand, strawberry or chocolate. Looking back I cannot believe how I could have been so simple. Nevertheless I was, and I decided I would prefer to have some strawberry ice cream and I went through the door where there were a whole lot of black people. Well this did not disturb me in any way and I went to the counter and everyone parted to let me get there and obviously everybody was looking wide-eyed at me. The counter man said brusquely, "I cannot serve you here." And I asked innocently, "Why not?" He said, "You have to go next door." Then of course I began to feel the strangeness of the environment but I still rather weakly said, "But I want strawberry ice cream." He said, "Go next door."

I slunk out of the place and went next door and found there I could get a total variety of ice-creams but they were meant in that section only for white people. I was absolutely horrified that such a situation should be prevalent, and disgusted with myself for being so idiotic and for never having realized during the period that I had been in the States that this situation was happening.

At that time you saw no colored faces in the magazines and no colored faced on the television. Blacks were almost an invisible race to white people: the most basic civil liberties withheld. I could not understand James' continued fascination with North America nor why he would wish to return to it. He told me, English people failed to consider it as the foreign country to them, which it was, even though the same language was spoken. I agreed with him.

In London, if James and I had been able to find a modest place to live and had the money to live by, my child, or our children, could have grown up without obstacles. In racist America, this was not possible. For the first time the black and white question would rear its beastly head. In Harlem, James would have been subject to insults as to why he could not find a black woman. In a white community, I would be ostracized, except say in sequestered walls of an university, for living with a black man.

James later married at different times, two white women, one in America and later one in England, both of them American. In what type of circumstances did they live? I am curious. I do not know. Surely neither lived with him in one room. They surely had better quarters. One of them had his son. I understand he has not fared too well. Was he sacrificed to politics? Both marriages broke up.

Now as an old woman, I am curious about them. I only know for certain that his wives were devoted to his politics, a matter of first importance. But what of his son? How did he bring him up? As I have written, James had this ideal of an "English Gentleman." I suppose in many ways I had the same. I would want my son as a man to be fair in his dealings with all people. That he would be "gracious" in his dealings with others, this coming from a high mindedness, a broad intellectual horizon and good education: that he would never act "like a cad" as my countrymen express it: most of all he would have integrity: integrity of mind as well as of action: never cheat or steal or act dishonorably. James' son could not have been brought up with such ideals.

By the Christmas 1940, I had been in the country for six months. I had only a visitor's visa for three months. This was easily renewable as I was a mother with a child and so was a refugee. But I had been working and I needed to go out of the country and re-enter with a work permit.

Some time earlier than James had left for the States, Esther Hieger, leaving her husband, had gone back to Canada with Earle Byrne. He had obtained his degree and now had a post as an assistant professor at Toronto University.

I had been in touch with her, during this time, and she had in each of her letters told me that if I ever wanted to go to Canada that I should come and stay with them. So now I wrote to her and asked if I might come up over the Christmas holidays, when I was free from work, and try to get my necessary working permit. She wrote back that she would be delighted. And so I made the preparations to go to Toronto from New York by train. We did not have a roomette, but I was able to at least get a sleeping car where we had a berth that my child and I would share. When we first arrived, Esther and Earle were quite enthusiastic about seeing me again and we talked about old times with Nello. However, they were not used to children. They had no children of their own, and a little toddler in the house created, I could see, a disturbance for them. It became quite plain that they were very unhappy in having us with them.

If I had been alone it would have been different, but the child complicated this situation for them. They had no idea of a child running freely through the house, and of a child who very active, wanting to explore everything and quite a menace who may break any small objects that are around. So Esther and Earle had to make re-arrangements in their home. And I knew after two days that even though they were not complaining, they were wishing that they had not asked me to visit with my son.

For themselves, they made no effort at Christmas festivities. They went out to see their friends. I excused myself from going because I knew I could not take the child. So our first few days became quite uneasy. The enthusiasm; with which they had sent their letters hoping to see me, were gone. When the child was in bed, we had drinks and talked about James and the group, and I told them about seeing him in Harlem, and that I understood that he was going off on a speaking tour of the American Trotskyists. To be able to do this, he must have used his phenomenal memory, so quickly to learn about American politics, because he had known little about them before he had left for the States.

While those few hours in the evening were very amiable after I had put my son to bed, they were short periods of the day. Earle and Esther would go out to see their friends with great relief and leave me in their house. I obviously could not leave the baby alone and I really was not so interested in trying to fit myself into their social life. So though they had been very warmly welcoming me before I arrived, this attitude changed within a few days. To make matters worse, my son who had been toilet-trained before we left England, was now bed wetting. Since they had no children this really shocked Earle and Esther. I had taken a plastic sheet with me but it still meant we had to change sheets every day, which was of course an imposition on my friends, unless they had themselves had children and understood the situation and the trauma of war for my son.

Then alas, my son became sick and came out in a rash. Esther took me with her to a local doctor and the man pronounced that my son had measles. For Esther and Earle this was the final stroke. Esther said they really could not have a child with measles at the house. She hustled about and the following day found a room where we could stay. This meant that my little boy and I were alone in Canada. The room was not very large, had a double bed which took up most of the space and had hideous wallpaper around the room, it was definitely quite confining and depressing especially since outside there were all the signs of Christmas festivities. I had to go to the American Consulate office to obtain my permit, but since it was Christmas, there were many days when the Consulate was shut, and so my son and I spent those days sitting alone in this confining and ugly small room. I think once or twice Esther put in a brief appearance to ask how we were. She did not want to go anywhere near my son since, neither she nor Earle had had measles and were afraid they might catch it.

My only desire was to get back to New York as soon as possible. Finally, all the forms were signed, and I received the necessary permit that I needed to return to the States and be able to work. It ended on December 31st, New Year's Eve. We got on the train which did not leave until late in the evening. I put my son to bed in his berth and once he was asleep, I thought; this is New Year's Eve, I must go to the bar and have a drink. I badly needed one. I had been through a particularly disappointing and tiring week, but when I went to the bar it was not open. There were Canadian restrictions on which hours the bar was to be open and even though this was New Year's Eve when I went, they were not serving drinks. So even foiled of this small support, I went back and went to bed and was glad to see the last of Canada and to arrive back in New York. At least there I had a place of my own and I had a bottle of Scotch in my apartment.

But I lived almost alone without companionship. I met other people seldom. Amongst those who came to the parties I had attended prewar with my husband was also John Strachey. He flirted at first with the left-wing, then quickly went over to the extreme right. His wife was one of the women who brought her children to the States. Occasionally we lunched together. I did not see her often but she was one of the few women I had known in London and now met again in New York. She wrote a book about the Cripps family taking it back to Sire Willmus Cripps who lived in the days of Robin Hood, and The Crusaders, who died in 1207 in Wessex, that part of England that today encompasses Gloucestershire and Oxfordshire, where my family roots were.

Early in 1941, I had a surprise visit from Charles Sumner, another member of the old group. I do not know how he had obtained my address, but I was very happy to see him. He asked me to go out with him to dinner. I told him I never went out in the evenings since I could not afford a baby-sitter. He brushed this aside, and I agreed to let him pay for one. We had a wonderful evening and for the first time I saw the lights of Broadway. I could not understand how he had been able to leave England, for he was young and healthy. It seems he had dual citizenship and held an American passport. For me it was a gay event going out, and to see an old comrade again. It was in distinct contrast to my visit to Esther and Earle.

James stayed in the United States long after his visa was functioning and the authorities were ready to deport him. For sometime he lived underground and managed to stay on for a considerable time, but in the end, they did deport him, first sending him to Ellis Island, to be imprisoned there. I do not know why he could not have received a working visa, when I was able to do so by going to Canada after six months, and obtaining it. Probably he could not do so because of his reputation already as a revolutionary figure and therefore, not one that was wanted in the country. Also, he had married an American woman which should have given him citizenship status.

By the early 1940's then, of the original members of the group that I had encountered at that first meeting, all were now all disbursed. Earle Birney, a Canadian, had gone back to Canada and was first an assistant professor of English, then a full professor. Esther Hieger had gone with him. Neither of them were in any way politically active after they had left. Earle continued with his literary work. He was a poet, and later became poet laureate of Canada under his real name of Earle Robertson. Esther, I gathered, now worked in activities on the university campus.

Some while later James was invited by a group of students at the University of Toronto to give a talk and paid for all his expenses. From one of those students, I learned that he never asked if Earle and Esther were still there, though they had been among his first and most ardent admirers. I thought it strange. After all, it was at the Hieger's house that we had first met. It was from that dinner party that James started his Trotskyist group in England. And it was with Esther that we had been to Paris together. In fact, I think that Esther had not only been one of his first admirers, but probably in love with him before she turned her attention to Earle Birney.

Both Gupta and Roy returned to India, and Gupta became a member of the Indian Parliament. Only Barbara, of those left behind in England, continued as a Trotskyist in the Labour Party.

Part Two
Separate Ways

8
Separate Ways: CLR

JAMES'S FIRST SOJOURN IN THE UNITED STATES LASTED FIFTEEN years from November 1938 until mid 1953. He went at the invitation of the Trotskyist Socialist Workers' Party. Through their organization, he went to the southern states and made speeches to the black cotton pickers for his first four months.

I knew about this because he sent me several letters during the eighteen months when he was in the States and I was still in England. Mail was slow from overseas during the period of the "phony" war, but it got through.

I sensed his great excitement especially about New York City. Five months after he arrived in New York he was invited by Trotsky, then in Mexico, to go with a group from the Socialist Workers' Party, for a meeting. Trotsky was particularly interested in the black movement in the United States; the question was discussed by his visitors. James was invited because he was a Negro. Trotsky felt he could inform him about the Negro situation in the United States.

But James was a West Indian, not an African American. He had not experienced what it meant to grow up a black man in North America. This, too, was 1939, when the black's civil rights were worse than they are today. Therefore, he could respond to Trotsky better than a white man but not as well as an American Negro. At that meeting, Trotsky suggested that James be given the task, for six months, of building a predominantly black group. When I saw him in September 1940, that is, eighteen months later, this task was impossible for James to have achieved. True, Marcus Garvey, born a Jamaican, had been successful, but he had lived for many years in the States, and his back-to-Africa movement had achieved considerable success. James was not in the same position, especially since he was obliged to work underground after his visa expired. When I met him he told me how much he had feared that the immigration authorities would catch up with him and deport him. That was in 1940.

The idea was to make this project part of the Trotsky movement and to entice not just black intellectuals, but also the black masses. James suggested that if Negroes wanted a form of self-determination, they should have it. However, he thought it unlikely despite his remoteness from them. His views were considered seriously, even though he was a Caribbean black man and not an American one. There is a difference.

James said: "I consider the idea of separation as a step backwards as far as a Socialist society is concerned. If the white workers extend a hand to the Negro, he will not want self-determination." A separate black state within the Union was being discussed at the time.

In 1936, the Committee for Industrial Organization (CIO), led by the fierce John L. Lewis, had formed a special Negro section. The Communist Party had organized the American Negro Labor Congress and the League for the Struggle for Negro Rights. Therefore, it seemed uncertain what role the Trotskyist could play in forming a new Negro organization. Nevertheless, there was general agreement that James and the others should return to New York and write an article about their views in their journal—an entire edition devoted to it—and that James should also try to organize a new black movement with the help of other black leaders. But no black mass group or party under James's leadership was ever formed. When I met him in New York, he never mentioned one, or an attempted one.

Actually, by the time his refurbished article on the subject was published in 1948, James had broken with the Socialist Workers' Party.

On returning from the meeting, James wrote a seventeen-page manuscript entitled *Preliminary Notes on the Negro Question*. He starts his article by saying "The 14 or 15 million Negroes in the USA represent the most militant section of the population. Economic exploitation and the crudest forms' of racial discrimination make this radicalism inevitable." Then he goes on to write: "For this we have historical proof . . . first in the part played by Negroes in the Civil War . . . and in response to Marcus Garvey." Later, he adds the Negro support and response to the Ethiopian question as evidence. This last point is somewhat doubtful. He berates the Communist Party on its Negro policies and then asks: What should a revolutionary party do?

James was addressing the members of the Trotskyist Socialist Workers' Party of the United States. There could not have been many blacks in the audience. He states that the SWP must (a) fight for the Negroes place and rights in the trade unions; (b) seek to make as many Negroes as possible members; (c) carry on a merciless struggle against white chauvinism.

But in (a), why did he confine himself to fight for negroes' rights in the trade unions? Surely also there were other Negro civil rights at that time in schools, housing, restaurants, buses, and so on, to be demanded.

Presumably, the SWP would have liked more black members, but they had only one in James, as we had only one, James himself, in London. Presumably, too, the SWP was already against white chauvinism.

James continued: "The great mass of Negroes are unorganized and no white party is going to organize them." In this he was correct.

Speaking tours to address blacks were only short forays during his life from 1938 to 1953, when he was deported. Fifteen years of his life were given over almost wholly to a group of a dozen or more white people interested in a reexamination of Marxist theory. True, he was later to write on the black question, but those immediate experiences, especially in Harlem, were not recorded. I would have expected that there would have been more anger in him on this subject. Yet Raya Dunayevskaya his colleague in the new Johnson Forest group thought he would become the leading black in the United States. But no organizing effort took place.

Instead of being dismayed by Harlem and its "mean streets," he seemed to have found pleasure in its vitality. He would go to performances at the Apollo Theater on 125th Street. He went to some of the dance halls, and though completely irreligious, he sometimes attended church services in the area. He met black intellectuals there, such as Richard Wright, the well-known black author.

The degradation of the ghetto seems to have evoked little anger in him. He thought the seething vitality would one day break out and, like a tidal wave, overwhelm white North Americans, forcing them to give blacks equality. Later, he moved to the Bronx, where blacks, Puerto Ricans and some whites lived. He went often to the movies.

As an old man in London, sick in bed, he would amuse himself by reading and watching soap operas. He liked the popular culture of the masses, whereas most intellectuals, including myself, are appalled by it, finding it the "circus" part of the "bread and circuses" of the Roman Caesars: a circus as bloodthirsty as throwing Christians to the lions or the fights of the gladiators. United States movies and television are full of violence: shootings and killings, smashing of cars, fires, sex, and killing.

There was no television when he and I were together in London.

We never listened to the radio together or went to movies. At that time, we feasted on talk, conversations about the classics, and stimulating discussions about politics and the conditions of the societies of the world.

It was two years in 1941 before the United States entered World War II, when blacks were kept in separate battalions and were given the most menial jobs and still discriminated against by whites, and there was the continued almost complete segregation of Negroes from the white population. It has always puzzled me how James dealt with this shock of the separation of the blacks and the whites. He himself lived and was working with a group of white people. He was the only black there as he had been the only black in the Trotsky movement in England. But the differences were great. He had to live in the ghetto. From Harlem he later moved to the Bronx. As far as I am aware, he never wrote of any bad experiences in Harlem nor wrote against the conditions that existed there. Yet he must have seen the children growing up in *Down Those Mean Streets,* of which my friend Piri Thomas was to write. I have not seen in any of James's works his cry for the salvation of those children of his race in the United States.

Oddly, he wanted to become a United States citizen. He wrote in *Amistad I,* published in 1970, on "The African Slave Trade and Slavery." This was a small paperback book in which several other blacks wrote. There was to be a series of them on African affairs and on black literature, but no more appeared after the first one. James had written and was coeditor in London, of the International African Opinion, in 1938, a journal of the International African Service Bureau. George Padmore was chairman and principally involved after he left the Communist Party.

Jomo Kenyatta, was the founder of the organization. He was wholly devoted to the African cause. James wrote only a few pieces for the journal between 1937 and 1938, that is, only during one year, because he left for the States in 1938.

When James was in the States, Trotsky brought up the question of the black movement there. James did not have much knowledge then of racism and could not relate to it in the same way as an African American brought up in North America. There was absolutely no way that his ideal of an English gentlemen could have even been understood by an American black. With such different roots, how could he have ever been a leader of blacks in the States? He could have been such a leader in the Caribbean, particularly in the West Indies.

He found North America foreign, though he was excited by it.

He said this was the only way for an English person to view it, even though they spoke the same language, or a slightly different colloquial form of that language. So he wrote to me to help in my adjustments.

James had as his role model, both as a young man and in his later years, a cricketer played mostly by an English gentleman.

He was not drawing crowds protesting against the war as he had in Trafalgar Square against that same war. He was not joining with any of the black movements springing up at that time. If he was still a revolutionary, he should have been speaking against the war and racial segregation. It was not until between his first and second period in the United States, however, that his interest and influence grew in the African black movement and in the West Indies. This was when his base was again in England.

He first met and became friendly with Nkrumah in the States. (Incidentally, Nkrumah sent me an invitation for the world wide meeting that he organized in Accra, Ghana, for peace.)

Marx, Engels, Hegel, Lenin, Trotsky—these were of primary interest to James, and the black movement was secondary, though he supported it. It is strange that he did not give himself wholeheartedly to his own native cause; or to the antiwar one.

When CLR had met with Leon Trotsky in Mexico at the April 1939 meeting, he had agreed to try and form such a movement; at that time he was not negative about it. James drafted a resolution on black liberalism for the Social Workers' Party that they accepted. But he was unsuccessful in forming any black organization. I do not think he ever tried to do so.

To a great extent, of course, these are not my memories of him but how I viewed his various activities after learning of them. I doubt that any of his London Trotskyist group would have favored his work in the Johnson-Forest Tendency.

Over the years, I had received the news that he had married twice. I was interested but not in any way affected by the news. However, in writing these memories of him, I became interested in how his wives and companions had managed to overcome the difficulties that we had. They were important ones of money; when James later returned to England, I have a report of his answering a question on this matter of who was supporting him. He said that Raya Dunayevskaya had tremendous influence on him and had found the means and if it had not been for her, he would have gone back to Great Britain. I do not think he would ever have let himself be dominated by a woman.

However, she said that he was the man to remain in the United

States, a black man who would automatically become the leader of the black movement, and because of his education, he could be head of the whole Trotskyist movement. Did he really believe he could oust such leaders as Max Schactman and Max Eastman as the U.S. Trotskyist heads?

He said that he was in doubt almost whether to go or to stay and Raya had insisted that he stayed. I quote him: "When I said I had no money to live on she said: 'Do not worry about money.'" She was reasonably well-off and had friends who would help him. So the problem that he had in London was solved by Gupta; in the States, it was removed by Raya Dunayevskaya's friends having sufficient personal income to support him: Lyman Paine and his wife supported him for twenty-five years in reasonable comfort. He had a key to their house and held his salonlike meetings there: a different setting from his London bed-sitting room.

My memories of James really end with my last meeting with him in Harlem in 1940.

It was after he had returned to England in 1953, roughly over a decade after our last meeting, that I began to get news about him fairly regularly from my friend Barbara and James himself. I write in another chapter of my contacts and correspondence with him over the years. It was during that first sojourn after our Harlem meeting that I lost touch. Then I began to hear from him and about him again, and so kept in touch, though infrequently, about what he was doing.

He suggests that if he had stayed in the States, the Johnson-Forest group would have grown to hundreds. In the speech that he gave when he was back in England, he also refers to his article on the United States Negro. He says Negroes would have formed part of his new organization after his first term of years in the United States.

I had shown myself I could live on limited means when I supported myself and my son in a modest walk-up apartment for six years. I could have been looked after as a refugee mother with a small child, but I chose otherwise. I could not understand James's having no qualms about accepting full support from others.

So James again was being financially supported by outsiders to pursue his work. So began the fully financially supported Johnson-Forest Tendency. Another woman, Grace Lee, soon joined them. She had a doctorate in philosophy and could translate German. The Russian-born Raya could translate the Russian. The money and the work being put into it resulted in only some self-printed pamphlets that they did not publish until 1950, nearly ten years after their formation.

Raya Dunayevskaya's further idea that James ought to become the black leader of the movement in the United States was high-flown. He was not a U.S. black; he had such a different background. If he was then going to try to bring the black masses into the new movement, the pamphlets produced were not ideas common to working-class people, but theses that were of interest only to intellectuals. I make these comments not because we were no longer together physically but because we had now parted ideologically.

James's group went back into the SWP in 1947 but broke away again by 1949. In 1950, he married Constance Webb, a young white American. They separated in 1955. He was then fifty-four and had not written another major book. He had produced a number of articles at that time but no volume such as *The Black Jacobins* or *World Revolution*. Most of his writings during this stay in the United States were articles or pamphlets that, though they, together with later works, were gathered into three books, were not the solid work of a single project. Only a limited number of these articles or pamphlets were about Africa and the Caribbean or the black question in general.

James suggested that he and his group of four, later twelve, were the only ones who had seriously gone into the philosophical analysis of the doctrines of Hegel and German philosophy. This was incorrect. There had been a number of such analysis especially by Europeans. Yet within the Socialists Workers Party and interested others, James and his colleagues were recognized as a newly formed group.

James and Raya Dunayevskaya became known as the leaders of the Johnson-Forest Tendency. At some point I was sent a Trotskyist paper called *Spartacus*. I had no idea who sent it to me. But *Spartacus* was the organ of a Trotskyist group, and they were arguing against this man, Johnson. I read it with some bewilderment because I became sure that Johnson was James—I had not known that he had adopted a pseudonym. I found myself agreeing with the Spartacus people and not with James and that of his new friend Forest.

James, now fifty years old, still had not received permission to stay in the United States. Because his wife, Constance Webb was an American, I thought that, through marriage he would obtained American citizenship. Evidently, this was not so. Or the FBI felt that he was an undesirable whom they did not want in their country, and he was sent to Ellis Island. This was very tragic for him, for he was not in good health, and under the circumstance in which he lived on Ellis Island, his health deteriorated further and more rapidly. In the end, he was deported back to England.

But while he was on Ellis Island, he again began corresponding with me. I learned of his Johnson-Forest period only later from reading about it. I had the feeling that it was at those times, when he was alone, that he would write to me and send me his books.

While James himself headed the group, he insisted that anyone who wanted to join had to work and to present a piece in writing. He said: "You will have to take a piece of Marxist writing, expound it and get it published even if it has to be published by us. Otherwise you cannot become a member of our party." This sounds somewhat fantastic to me. This was to be a *Workers'* movement?

I seem to be critical of what was James doing in all these years into his middle age, for it seems that if he had had a single goal in mind from the beginning, he could have achieved it. He was a man of such tremendous abilities. Looking at it now from a distance of years, it seems he dissipated his efforts during what should have been the most productive period of his life.

The pamphlets that the three or four people published at their own expense during the seven years with him were: *Notes on Dialectics* at first published in mimeographed form then later as a book; *State Capitalism and World Revolution* written by the group and published in 1950; *Facing Reality*, also written by the group and published in 1958.

None of these works with limited circulation in any way helped the black movement. James had not become a national black leader as had been predicted. He was fifty-two when he was deported to Ellis Island. He had, during the war years, gone back to the South to work as an agitator against the war among black workers, but because he had to conduct his activities "underground," they were severely limited.

When he returned to England, while the new generation of Trotskyists were interested in him, no formal group was created around him. Also he now no longer had any source of financial support. *The Manchester Guardian* luckily gave him back his job as a cricket reporter. This would lead, in turn, some years later, to his writing *Beyond a Boundary,* a book about cricket, interspersed with philosophical reflections in general, and about famous West Indian cricketers, in particular.

This again was more of a cultural rather than a political work. Unless *Mariners, Renegades and Castaway,* which he wrote on Ellis Island, is considered a political allegory, he had not written a book or pamphlet on politics since he had collaborated with others in the Johnson-Forest group. He had not written a book alone on political subjects since he wrote *The Black Jacobins* and *World Revolution, 1917–1936,* when I was with him in the thirties in London.

In 1970, he sent me a copy of *Amistad I*. This was a book of essays by black writers and more were supposed to appear. This did not happen. James's contribution was *The Atlantic Slave Trade and Slavery*. He felt it would remind me of *The Black Jacobins*, a book I had helped him with. It is a good, interesting article of some forty pages.

It was after he had returned to England in 1953, that is, over a decade after our last meeting, that I would get news about him fairly regularly while he was there, from my friend, Barbara.

I write in another chapter of my contacts and correspondence with him over the years. It was during that first sojourn after our Harlem meeting that I lost touch. Then I began to hear from him and about him again, and so kept in touch, though infrequently, about what he was doing.

In 1958, after twenty-five years away, James decided to return to Trinidad. A group of West Indians had gathered around him in London. Dr. Eric Williams invited him to edit his party's journal. But it was far too late for James to have gone back. He gave a series of lectures in the capitol and became, as requested, editor of *The Nation*, a new name he gave the party paper. But it was not a revolutionary paper as *Fight* had been, but a literary one. This was the official journal of the People's National Movement. His people had not forgotten him, but he had been out of touch too long. He had not participated in the fight for independence, so he was a late comer. It became necessary for him politically to challenge Williams, but it was too late. He had been known earlier as a coming writer and not as a political figure.

James had to leave after this short foray. The battle, however, remained in his mind, and three years later he returned. Williams knew the threat to his power that James might be. Immediately, he put him under house arrest, then, having shown his authority, released him.

This was in 1965. Elections were to be held in 1966. James decided to challenge Williams for the head of government. He formed a party of his own, calling it The Workers' and Farmers' Party, greatly helped by George Weeks who was a leader of the Oilfield Workers' Trade Union. In fact, without the partnership of Weeks, there could have been no serious party.

The challenge was made much too late. James had become an outsider who had not fought in the struggle for self-determination on the island. He had written briefly about it but from far off. Naturally he lost the election, receiving only 2 percent of the votes, and when this happened, he again left the island and returned to England.

The lectures he had given in Port of Spain were published earlier as a small book under the title of *Modern Politics* (he sent me a copy). Back in London in 1962, he wrote another pamphlet, *Party Politics in the West Indies*.

Nevertheless, when he again might have returned and offered leadership was before the Black Power Revolt that occurred in 1970, he did not do so. It involved the black workers, a section of the military (vitally important) and peasants.

Also what was quite remarkable was that the Negro workers marched miles to the East Indian farm workers to get them to join the revolt. There had been antagonisms previously between the two groups. Students joined the great demonstration too. Placards were carried lauding the Black Panthers and such United States black leaders as Malcom X, Stokely Carmichael, and Eldridge Cleaver. C. L. R. James's name was not among them. Leaders somehow sprang up spontaneously, but there was no revolutionary party organizing it.

There were banners proclaiming, "King Sugar: Black blood; black sweat: black tears; white profits." It was called the February Revolution, and it had begun on the first and second day of Carnival. Why was James not there when a revolution was taking place on his own island? It was just four years since he had been there challenging the prime minister, whose caricature was carried by the marchers.

Why had his sojourn to Trinidad left so little trace in such a short time? Perhaps if he had gone back earlier, he could have taken part in it. The popular, spontaneous movement was, of course, suppressed. James's co-worker in the Farmers' and Workers' Party, George Weeks, was imprisoned. Perhaps James would have been as well. Perhaps if he had been there, his presence might have made a difference.

Grace Lee had known Nkrumah. He was then a young man studying in Lincoln, Pennsylvania. She arranged a meeting between the two men, and from that time on, the two were in touch with each other. However, it was Grace Lee, who mostly kept up the correspondence. When Nkrumah decided to go to England, James gave him a letter of introduction to George Padmore. He wrote that the young African needed political training. Padmore, as the head of the International African Service Bureau in London, was glad to given Nkrumah all the help he could before he returned to Ghana. Nkrumah became head of the Convention People's Party, and after elections in 1957, he became prime minister of the first independent African state.

For his inauguration, he invited both James and Padmore to be there. James went eagerly. He said, at the time, that he was more interested in Africa than in the Caribbean. For his part, Nkrumah was glad to have such a fine orator at his disposal. James gave speeches in both the Gold Coast and in Nigeria, which he believed was the birth place of his ancestors. He returned to England and found that he had been asked to give some lectures at the Federal City College (afterward the University of the District of Columbia). For this he was given a new visa to enter the United States. He gladly went back and lectured at many colleges in the United States.

At the time, the idea of uniting all the nations of Africa was a popular one. There had already been five conferences supporting this idea. In 1974, James and others would call for a Sixth Pan-African Congress. It took place, but James, at the last minute, declined to attend. The African leaders were mainly interested in their regional independence. He was more interested in the union of the whole continent.

When he had been in England in the sixties, he had published *Beyond A Boundary,* with which he was to achieve fame when a second edition was printed in 1982. By that time he had celebrated his eightieth birthday. Also, his relationship with his third wife, Selma Weinstein, ended, though they never divorced. By his first wife, he had had a son, nicknamed Nobby, but because of his exile and divorce, he saw little of his son. His last days were spent in Brixton, London, where he had a group of new admirers around him, and where he died when he was almost ninety years old.

It had been a long life, full of different activities in diverse fields, and though as in most people's lives, there had been ups and downs, I think he died happy.

9
Separate Ways: LLC

THIS BOOK IS FOR PEOPLE INTERESTED IN C. L. R. JAMES. I FEEL justified in briefly talking about myself, however, about my life after my relationship ended with him, because in knowing something about my own life the reader can get an indication of the type of man that James was.

All of James's women were white, middle class, well read, and intelligent. Since the others have not written their stories, each of which would make an interesting book, I have written mine. I was hesitant at first because I did not want it to sound somewhat like writing for *True Confessions*. However, at my age, it has given a certain point to my days to look back to that love affair in my youth and remember also how and when there had been other points of contact between James and myself in the intervening years.

I started my career in the United States as a publicity writer for *Bundles of Britain,* an organization that was, at that time, sending mostly bundles of clothes to refugees in England, particularly to the children. At that early time someone steered me toward the English Speaking Union with its headquarters on Fifth Avenue. I imagine that someone at the union must have told me about *Bundles of Britain,* I was the only Englishwoman working there.

The English-Speaking Union received a visit from the Duke and Duchess of Windsor when they came to the United States. There was a little girl who was to give a bouquet to the Duchess, and my son was to accompany her. Since he was so small, I had to go behind my son and steer him straight. I had found a little shirt that had his name stitched on it, and I let him wear it that day. I have never liked the Duchess of Windsor. I think she should have been prepared, if she really loved Edward, to have been his known "special friend." She would have had a better life and would have been accepted within a wider group of people than she ever had been as the Duchess of Windsor. Nevertheless, after the little girl had given her the bouquet, the Duchess crouched down and put her finger over my son's name on his shirt and said, "So, this is your name?" He looked at her without any idea of what she was saying, but I thought it was gracious, and an unbending attitude on her part. The Duke of Windsor, however, stood a little apart and looked extremely bored.

My next venture was to go to the British War Relief. I suggested to them that I publish for them a magazine that they would distribute to all their branches. They thought about it and decided to do it. So I started getting some compelling photographs on the bombing of London. I received some from a newspaperman friend there. He sent me some very fine ones. I decided to call the magazine *Salute,* that is, a salute to the heroism that was happening in Britain, even though I was antiwar. This was, after all, a relief organization to help those who had been damaged and hurt in the war and by the bombings. I got Gertrude Lawrence, then in New York, to write a rather lightweight piece, and then I got Andre Maurois to write an article. He asked me to tea at the Waldorf Towers. While I was there he said, "You know, I had to leave France with nothing. I am an absolute refugee." I looked around his living room and I felt: "Well you are a very lucky refugee" and "Living in such surroundings is not my idea of someone in that category."

Then, I wrote to my old friend Bertrand Russell in Pennsylvania. He had been, as I have mentioned, a pacifist in the First World War. However, he was convinced this time that it was a fight against Fascism, and he wrote a perfectly somber and in no way controversial article for me. But the Committee of the British War Relief decided they could not have an article by a man such as Bertrand Russell in the magazine. I was not only very upset, but also ready to resign at once. Not resigning is one of the nonactions that has pricked my conscience ever since. However, I was alone and had a baby to look after, and in the end I wrote him a very apologetic letter. Later on when I was in touch with him again, I told him how all through the years it had been on my conscience. But he responded that he understood what the situation had been. He was anathama at the time in the press because of his views on sex. He came up from Pennsylvania to New York, and I remember waiting at Pennsylvania Station and then seeing him come up the ramp. He took me to have lunch, and then afterward we discussed what he should write. To have to return his article was a very sorry business. But we had a very pleasant afternoon.

By the end of the year when the United States went to war, December 1941, the British War Relief stopped. Americans had their own organization for the United States to support. But French Relief was still running. This was mostly for the prisoners of war and for children. I felt I could support that, so I applied for a job. It was being run by Anne Morgan, J. P. Morgan's sister, a very autocratic woman who took a liking to me. She made me her promotion director. I used to drive around in a big car with a mink's tails wrap over my knees. During the day I would go to the Plaza Hotel with her to have lunch and then in the evening pay five cents to go back home on the subway or bus. It was quite a contrast in types of living.

While I worked with Anne Morgan, I had several prominent volunteers, such as Schiaparelli and Mme. Clemenceau, to help me. Andre Maurois turned up again, too. We did a number of promotions, and as sort of alter-ego of Anne Morgan, I was introduced to all the people who came to see her. We ran several films to raise money, and I met many famous people, such as Jean Gabin and Charles Boyer, who James was to describe to his next wife as being a great lover.

During the time I was with the organization, 1941-42, there was a Swedish woman who worked there. We became friends. When the summer arrived, she suggested we take a cottage on Long Island. She had a daughter and I had a son, and we could hire a maid to come in daily to look after them. Her husband was a Russian named Romanoff. He had a friend, another Russian, who rented my apartment for the summer and also came to see us on weekends. My early social isolation was ending.

When I was still with Anne Morgan, my first book about babies, *Your First Baby,* was published by A. S. Barnes. I had noticed in the telephone listings that there was a magazine of a similar title, so I decided to visit the publisher. He was looking for an editor for the magazine. I told him not only about the book but of my own experience as an editor in London of *The Nursery World.* He asked me if I would like to edit his magazine.

So I began editing the new magazine. About two years later, I decided that I could easily publish my own magazine. All I had to do was to get orders from the manager of one of the large amalgamated department stores and ask if they would be interested. They told me to bring back a dummy of the magazine as I conceived it. I had met a young light-skinned negro who was an layout artist, and he agreed to make the dummy for me. So began my publishing career. I continued with the magazine for a long while. During this period I also started a second magazine, a slick one costing fifty cents, a fair amount at that time. Later, I was able to interest the people at *Pocketbooks* to distribute the magazine.

I had always been interested in the upbringing of children. Children have no votes and few advocates. The first pages of my slick four-color magazine was devoted to reprinting *The Declaration of the Rights of Children* by the United Nations. The magazine had a quarter of a million circulation. I wrote editorials and had sympathetic doctors expound the views of Dr. Benjamin Spock, Bertrand Russell, and John Dewey. I had known all three, and their views had greatly influenced me. All were similar in the stands they took on education and the role of parents in children's lives. Dr. Spock's book, written later than when I first knew him, became the Bible of middle-class parents.

So I continued for some years working on my second interest, children and their education. I would have preferred to have been writing politics, my politics. But this was second best, and I had to earn a living.

It was at some point around this time that I saw James again. One day to my astonishment he poked his head into my office, but after seeing I had a visitor, he disappeared. This must have been some time in the early forties, at time when the Johnson/Forest Tendency was already in operation. But it only amounted to one startled look at him. He still, of course, looked much the same as I had seen him in Harlem. I do not know why he did not wait to see me. I was disappointed. It would have been good to chat with him. He had gone first to an upper floor where the young Negro was doing the layout for the magazine.

Soon, I decided that we would have a television program for the magazine. I became moderator, and we had a number of interesting people on the program. At first I did it live, and then it was taped on Channel 13 and appeared at midday on Saturday mornings. When on tape, the show followed Mike Wallace at the studio. Dr. Baumgartener, head of Planned Parenthood was one of the guests, but he was not allowed to talk about birth control.

Finally, the pressure of running two magazines, a TV show, a household, and looking after my son proved too much for me, and I had my first serious heart attack. All this time I had been writing weekly to my husband, and he would regularly write back. However, one weekend after I had been alone for four years, one of the other women with children, who had come over on the boat with me, invited me for a weekend at her cottage. She had a guest staying with her, a rather pleasant man, and he offered to drive me and my son home. From that moment we became friends. His wife had been in an asylum for five years, and he had just obtained his divorce. He had two children, and on Saturdays we would take his two children and my son to the zoo and then have lunch at the open-air restaurant. After a while we became lovers. The affair was rather difficult, however, because he could not come to my small apartment with my son there, and he lived with his mother and his two children on West Side Drive, so our meetings occurred infrequently. However, we had lunch together almost daily at a little French restaurant just off Fifth Avenue. I told him all about myself and he told me about himself. He had been born in South Africa and then had gone to Oxford to receive his degree. Then, during the war, he came to the States, more or less at the same time as I had. He had brought his two children and his mother. He then want to Harvard and became a lawyer under the tutelage of Felix Frankfurter. Since he was not a British citizen, he was able to leave England. As a Jew, of course, it was very important for him to escape. He came from an enormously wealthy family. But I would never let him help me financially. I was as independent as when I was with James.

At the end of the war, in 1946 my husband arrived from England. Unfortunately, just before he arrived I received an anonymous letter telling me that he had been living with a woman and had two children by her. He did not stay with me but with a woman writer, a well-known one, Kay Boyle. He wanted us to renew our relationship. The letter I had received, however, had upset me, and I felt that he should go back to the woman who had had his two children because it would be very difficult for her to be alone.

My husband was extremely angry that I knew, and I told him about the anonymous letter. He said it made no difference and that he wanted me. I felt he should return to England. At the same time, my new lover wanted me to marry him. I thought back to the days when James had been my lover and how understanding my husband had been and we had gone back together again. He had still been very caring all the time that I had had the affair with James and had written me loving letters over the six years we had been apart.

From editing *Fight* with James in London, I had learned about the history and politics of Palestine. (As early as November 1938, *Fight* had an article on British terrorism in Palestine.) Great Britain had received Palestine as a mandate from the League of N..tions in 1922. The Jews accepted the idea of two states: a Jewish state and a Palestinian state. But the Palestinians were militantly opposed to carving up their country. The United Nations established a special committee that proposed a plan to divide Palestine into a Jewish state, an Arab state, and a small international zone including Jerusalem.

The British High Commissioner and British troops withdrew, and on May 14, 1948, the state of Israel was proclaimed. On the same day, it received de facto recognition from the United States. Fighting began immediately and continued until a truce was enforced by the United Nations Security Council (composed of representatives of only the seven great powers). Israel was invited to join the United Nations after the Israelis elected a parliament with Ben Gurion as prime minister. The British with their mandate had been the prime movers in carving up Palestine. The British army gave the Israelis arms, and it was the British army that had demolished Arab villages and hundreds of peasant dwellings and killed the villagers and set up concentration camps. All this was in support of the new country of Israel.

In addition to my husband, who still had a strong attraction for me and my wealthy Jewish friend, I was also being courted by a Russian who had attended and taught at Harvard. After teaching at Harvard for a couple of years, he went to work at an engineering firm. He, too, wanted to marry me, though we never had been lovers. I was really in a turmoil. Here were three men who wanted to marry me, and I was torn between them. I broke out in a very bad case of hives around my waist and had to go to a doctor. The doctor asked me what was making me nervous. He felt that the hives were due to nervousness, and I told him, "Three men want to marry me and I do not know whom to marry." He roared with laughter. He said: "Most women would be flaunting the fact that there were three men who wanted to marry them and instead of that you are troubled and get the worst case of hives I have seen in a long while."

The Israeli was out of the question, though, undoubtedly, I would have enjoyed being the wife of an ambassador, but I could not be a Zionist, not in Palestine. With such knowledge as I had had about Palestine, and from my Trotskyist past with James, I could not associate myself with Israel. Trotsky was a Jew, but he was anti-Zionist. My husband was the father of my child; hence, I was very torn about the situation. Furthermore, we liked each other very much; we got along very well; the same things amused us; we had a similar set of mind, and, of course, we both had literary ambitions. So we could be together again as a couple of writers. Writing had been in my thoughts for a long time.

Meanwhile, my Jewish lover was becoming very important in Israel. He was made the first Israeli consul-general in New York and then the first ambassador to the United Nations. This was before Golda Meir or Eban Iban. In his new position he sometimes would take me to the restaurant in the United Nations. He introduced me to Dag Hammerskold, who, after we had had a friendly but brief chat, addressed me as the man's wife. I told him that I was not his wife but the ambassador wanted to marry me. A friend of his, another lawyer, came to me and told me how he needed a wife in his new position to act as a hostess for him; that he had to have a hostess; that he was sure I would make a most admirable one, and that, of course, he was in love with me. Later on my friend became the first ambassador for Israel to Canada and subsequently, Israeli ambassador to England. The problem was that I could not possibly accept a Zionist husband.

I finally decided to settle down with my gentle, civilized Russian, who, because his mother had been a university professor, believed in the equality of women. I had become extremely indignant by that time of the crucifixion of liberals by Senator Joseph McCarthy. I decided that there surely must be something that I could do in protest. I had lunch with a woman friend who was politically wise about politics in the United States. I was now newly married and living on Long Island. She was my next door neighbor. My new husband and I had stayed in New York City for a while, but the school my son had attended ended when he was eight. We decided it would be best to bring him up in the country, or rather in the suburbs, because we were both working. We started by renting a small cottage on Long Island, then bought a lovely old house on the waterfront.

Until then I was English. I had never thought of changing. I asked my friend how McCarthy could be stopped. She said that he could be stopped by getting control of the country through the Democratic Party. Adlai Stevenson was about to run as the next Democratic presidential candidate. I immediately became a United States citizen; otherwise, I would not have been able to act. I began what was my only political activity in America. I formed an Adlai Stevenson Club.

The club was in Suffolk County, a Republican stronghold. Its purpose was to discuss all topics covered by the election, but I let it stray far beyond this. I brought in Norman Thomas to speak on socialism. He and I had become friends since we often traveled on the Long Island Railroad together. After reading our newspapers, we would start discussing the day's news. Sometimes we agreed, sometimes not, since I stood to the left of him. He was happy to come and talk to my group. He ran several times for president on the socialist ticket. Also, I asked someone from the NAACP to address us. He talked about the Negro problem and racism. If there were any Negroes in our town, they were hidden. Some of my group were a little wide-eyed at my selection of speakers, but all found them stimulating, and the series provided new ideas for them and I hope made them more politically aware.

Then I opened local headquarters throughout the county. I enjoyed being politically active once again. Though these were not my politics, I felt that fighting Senator McCarthy was worth it. It was during the McCarthy era that James was incarcerated on Ellis Island prior to his deportation from the United States, a move that he was fighting. So without being aware of it until he started to write me from there, I was once again fighting with him in a cause. And once more I became a speaker as in our Trotskyist days in England.

Although I had not his power of speaking, still I believe we made progress for the Democrats in an almost 100 percent Republican area. There was a local Democratic Party, but I was told by a writer for *The New York Times* that they had sold out to the local powers for some small quid pro quo. This was disheartening. They were mostly women in the small group that I gathered around me to work the various sections of the county, liberal middle-aged women who were glad for a chance to be active to give point to what were mostly boring days in fairly well-to-do milieus. And for me, it was good to feel that I had not lost some of those skills that I had learned with James in our London days, when we were both newcomers to a political ambience.

As I look for the thread throughout my life that may give it a pattern, I believe that it started with that child who looked as if she had all the worries of the world on her shoulders, because she felt someone had to—the child who was molded by soberly reading all Charles Dickens's books that treated the lives of poor people and the whole terrible underworld of poverty, especially about children; the young girl who wrote her own sad stories so that those reading them would all become good; the timid young girl who could write *Murderess* on the blackboard of the classroom to protest the harassment of another girl; the young girl who doubted the goodness of God, since He allowed so much pain in the world.

Soon after my first marriage, my husband and I formed a foursome with a young Welshman, Jon Evans, and his wife. We were not consciously political, we were socialistic rather than socialists. Three of us planned to be writers. We had many evenings of discussion. We had all been born in the first decade of 1900 and felt we represented the young people of the century. I suggested that we should publish a journal. The others thought it was a good idea. We decided to produce a dummy. My husband did the layouts. The format was large, 12×15, with a heavy, medium-green paper cover well designed. Three of us wrote the articles. We called the journal *Twentieth Century* or some similar title. As far as I can remember, none of us had read Marx and his maxim "to each according to his needs and to each according to his abilities." Our ideas dealt with the world, the many nations, and not individuals. We thought each country should produce according to the best of its abilities, its resources, and its population and that there should be a worldwide sharing and distribution among all countries.

Our effort looked professional when completed. The young Welshman said we must now find a sponsor. He suggested he should call on H. G. Wells. This he did, and Wells, after some consideration, said that he would support our efforts. There were several meetings with Wells. I had always been an admirer of his and very much wanted to meet him. After all, it had been my idea. But Jon Evans kept us away from the famous writer. I was hurt and disappointed. I should have loved to have talked to Wells about all my ideas at that time, but I lacked the aggressiveness to insist that I and the others share in the meetings with Wells. Wells paid for the printing and introduced the journal to a magazine distributor. We published three issues of a quarterly, but the time was not sufficient for the magazine to be successful.

It was after the magazine folded that I went into the Trotskyist group.

When I later formed my own Adlai Stevenson group in Suffolk County, Long Island, I did so mainly as a counterreaction to McCarthyism.

I was asked to go as a delegate to the Democratic Convention in Chicago and to Adlai Stevenson's party there. Unfortunately and regretfully, I could not go due to the pressures of work.

10
Contacts and Correspondence

I HAD BOTH CORRESPONDENCE AND CONTACTS WITH JAMES OVER A number of years. I will try to set these down in chronological order.

First, there is the report about me in the letter he wrote to Constance Webb, his wife-to-be. His chronicler puts this at 1944, that is, four years after I had last seen him, seven years since we had been lovers. It was a long time for him to still be thinking of me.

During the Johnson-Forest period, I received a copy of *Spartacus*. On second thought, I believe James must have sent it to me without a note, perhaps to let me know his present political position. This must have been late in the forties. I do not know anyone else who could have sent it to me. I had no other Trotskyist contact in the States.

My views coincided with those of *Spartacus*, since I had remained a Trotskyist.

Then I received a letter from him when he was on Ellis Island. He told me of his writing about *Moby Dick*. This had been a work he had wanted to do for a long time. He had talked to me about it in our London days. He also wrote how ill he was with his ulcer.

Once he was back in England, in the next five years, in the fifties—I received letters from him. Also, my woman friend and I had continued to write, and though I sensed a reluctance on her part, she would let me know that he asked her to send me his love. She and her husband came to see us while we were living on Long Island, and again through them I heard further news of James.

Her husband had become a businessman. However, Barbara continued to work in the Labour Party as a Trotskyist. She, more than her husband, saw James, and he explained to her his break with Trotskyism, his Johnson/Forest group's political positions, and how he would like to return to the United States. She too found this strange and felt he was better situated in England.

She was interested, but disapproving, that we still occasionally wrote to each other.

There was to be an encounter later about which I write, in which she played a decisive and negative role.

A contact that might have occurred but didn't was one I learned about recently.

During the war and before my second marriage, my son and I had gone for summers to a house on the waterfront of Huntington. Later, my husband and I would have a different house on the same waterfront. Huntington, Long Island, is adjacent to Northport. James spent many weekends in the forties with his friends, Freddie and Lymen Paine, in Northport. It meant that we were looking out on the same stretch of water just a few miles away from each other probably on many occasions. We also went to Northport, ten minutes away by car, on many occasions. James is equally likely to have gone to Huntington, so we could have met.

When James returned to England after his U.S. sojourn, Barbara and her husband linked up with him again. The remnants of our group had moved into the Labor Party before I left. She continued her membership all her life until she died in late 1988. I had had a letter from her that she had planned to visit me in January 1989. Alas, she died before she made the visit.

I was grief stricken when I learned of her death. Our meeting would have been very enjoyable. There was much to relate about those long intervening years since we had last met. There was much she would have contributed to my poor memory of the past that we had shared. Though she had this curious anger about my love affair with James, we had been friends for many, many years. She would have been able to give me firsthand knowledge of him while he was in England. I did learn that he had divorced Constance Webb and married another American woman.

I imagine that James knew when she wrote to me and vice versa. I am sure that each time he would have sent his love but that she would not always have passed that on. I could never fathom why she had this strong antagonism about my relationship with him.

I flew to England in 1963. My husband and I had sailed to the Soviet Union from Montreal. After a few days of marveling at the treasures of that beautiful "Venice of the North," we flew to Moscow, where he still had two sisters, whom he had not seen for over fifty years. Unfortunately, he contracted pneumonia while there. He had toured Moscow with a young nephew whom he had not previously met and he had not dressed warmly. The young man enthusiastically took him to see some of his favorite places and this had obviously overtired him. His lungs had never been good.

By 3:00 A.M. his temperature had risen to 103° F. Speaking no

Russian, but holding the thermometer in my hand, I went along the corridor to the old woman who presided over the rooms on that floor. Holding out the thermometer to her, I said, "moi mousse," meaning, "my husband." This was one of the few Russian words I had learned. She questioned me, and I guessed she was asking me his nationality, words that were easy to understand meant "French" or "German."

I shook my head and pleased with myself said, "Americanski."

She had, by this time, telephoned to an outside headquarters and continued to question me, repeating my answers into the telephone. We managed further with sign language. She pointed to her stomach, I shook my head. She pointed to her head. I shook my head. I pointed to my chest and coughed vigorously. She interpreted this into the telephone.

Within fifteen minutes a doctor and attendant arrived. My feminine sensibility was gratified because the doctor was a woman and the attendant a young man. They had an ambulance waiting below to take my husband to a hospital.

I offered her a pencil and paper, and indicated I wanted to know where my husband was being taken. After he left, I started to cry because my head was filled with cold war stories.

The floor attendant arrived. She pulled me to her buxom bosom and patted me, undoubtedly saying sympathetically in her own language, "There, there, my dear. It is going to be all right."

I walked the floor till six A.M., then called my husband's sister. I had learned to say "Gorod" into the telephone, meaning one wanted a number within the city, then give the number. I never found any difficulty making telephone calls.

My sister-in-law was upset to hear the news. She said she would rush over to the hospital, then fetch me later.

I will not digress further by describing the hospital; actually, it was within a compound of hospitals. It was clean, functional, and not fancy in any way, but my husband had very good care.

I decided, again under the influence of cold war propaganda, that I should go to the American Embassy and inform them my husband was in a hospital.

I was taken to the office of a young man, who immediately telephoned for a supervisor.

They took me to task asking me why I had not registered with them earlier.

"I did not know I had to," I said. They then made the preposterous suggestion that I should remove him from the Russian hospital and fly him back to the United States.

I was not impressed by their attitude and was certainly not going to follow their advice and remove him from the Moscow hospital, where he seemed content and was being well cared for, and, incidentally, without charge.

Their way was a sure way to kill my husband. I assured them I was confident that he was getting good care. They told me that the Soviet hospitals tended to keep patients longer than necessary. I told them that as soon as he was convalescing, I'd fly to England and leave him behind. I wanted them to know where he was.

As soon as my husband was in the hospital, all of his newly found relatives came flocking to see him. I would sit in a corner while they talked in Russian, and he seemed very happy to be back with his family again. It seemed silly for me to remain in Moscow, where I was going back alone each evening to the Hotel Berlin. I was not able to do anything more for him, and he obviously had plenty of family to look after him. We had intended to spend two weeks of our vacation in Moscow, and two weeks in England. I wanted to see my family, so we now arranged that I was to go on without him, and as soon as he was well, he would join me. When I got back, I was picked up by my nephew who lived near London.

While there, I called my friend, Barbara, in Welwyn Garden City, to tell her that I was in England. She was very excited and pressured me to say I would come and stay with her for a couple of days. My whole visit was going to be brief, and I had to see my sister. However, I said that I would come for two days. After we had made these arrangements, she came over one morning and whisked me back to her home, chatting furiously as she drove a little wildly back to her home. She had invited two other friends with whom I had been very close, and with whom, all through the years, I have kept up a correspondence. One of the friends was ill and could not come. The other, my dear Jamaican friend, arrived, and we had a very congenial lunch together.

After the Jamaican friend left, Barbara's husband came home. He also had been at the university with us, then had been one of the group when I was in London. Now that James was back in England, they had both joined with him again. Oddly, however, they never mentioned James. I was curious and would like to have known what was happening with him. They were seeing him, but infrequently. They should have told me. They both seemed to prefer to keep silent about him. However, we spent a very pleasant evening together. The next morning again rather oddly, my friend said she had to go shopping and thought that I would prefer to amble about the city and see how much of it I remembered. I knew this would be enjoyable, but since we had so little time together, I thought this rather odd also, not to spend the hours together. So I took my walk along the old streets with which I had been familiar. The little town seemed much as I remembered it, but more green. When I had left, many of the trees had been newly planted and were now full grown. It was a lovely day, and walking along those pavements, among once familiar houses, I grew nostalgic for England, my green and pleasant island. For this was summer, and a fine day in England is hard to duplicate. I found the house I had lived in, though I wandered around a little before I discovered it, but it was not much different from when I had left. The shrubbery we had planted was now fully grown, and the house and doors had been painted a different color; but it was still as I remembered it. I saw the path leading from the house to the small gate out of which my son, pushing his toy dog, and I had left to go to the Western world.

I knew that I had changed since I had left. I wondered how different my life would have been if instead of going to the United States, I had gone, as my sister-in-law had done, to Cornwall and escaped the ravages of the German bombings and, what seemed to be the likelihood at the time, the German occupation. I knew that that somewhat shy young woman had become more sophisticated by living in New York City. Nevertheless, there have always been inexplicable periods or moments of shyness that descend on me that are part of my English upbringing.

I went back and Barbara and I had tea together, chatting very amicably. It was not until after dinner when her husband had returned home that Barbara told me they would be going out for their usual bridge night. Again, I was rather astounded. It seemed a little odd, since we had so short a time together, for her to be leaving me alone. They had not, as I said, mentioned James, although they knew I must have been curious and interested to hear about him. Since he had returned to England, they were seeing him, but infrequently. She had told me that his American wife was living with him. However, as they were going out the door, Barbara thrust a piece of paper in my hand and said, "Here is James's telephone number. He asked that you should call him." This all seemed somewhat abrupt.

It was then about seven o'clock in the evening. I went to the telephone and dialed the number she had given me. A woman who answered the telephone sounded very pleased and told me, when I said who I was, that James had been waiting eagerly for my call. She sounded very pleasant and friendly. So James came to the telephone—I had not heard his voice in over twenty years. He was very upset that I had not called sooner. He said, "I am very sick but I intended to come and see you. I have been waiting since yesterday for you to call me." I told him that I had only just been given his telephone number and had called him at once. He was very upset and said he had been so much looking forward to our meeting. I would have, of course, enjoyed it too, and found it rather odd and a little cruel that Barbara had not given me his telephone number earlier. She had always been so strongly against our relationship. But over twenty years had passed. Did she still believe that he and I, once we placed our hands together, would jump into the nearest bed? I could not fathom her reasons.

James and I had a long, long, long talk on the telephone. It was not what we should have had—a whole long evening together and alone—since Barbara must have known that she and her husband had intended to play bridge. We did at least have the opportunity of speaking together. He told me all about his ulcer, which had bothered him for so much of his life, and how sick he was feeling at the moment. But he again assured me that he would, nevertheless, have journeyed out for the pleasure of seeing me and of having some full hours to catch up with what we had done with our lives since we last parted.

James was particularly angry about it. He said: "I am quite sick but I would have made the journey to see you." He asked if I could not extend my visit. But all plans had been made for me to spend the next two days with my sister. Barbara and my nephew were to meet halfway, to shorten the journey for each, to take me to Suffolk. Also, I was in no way sure my friend would even agree to the suggestion. She had seen that Nello and I did not meet, so she was unlikely to make new arrangements so that we could.

It was very disappointing for us both. It would have been a wonderful evening of memories, just the two of us together again alone.

Since I had just come from the Soviet Union, naturally I told James about that and about the experiences that my husband and I had had while we were there. I said that I thought that the Soviet Union had become in the towns a country of petit-bourgeoisie, that the people were looking for more varied and better consumer goods, and that it was heavily burdened by an overwhelming bureaucracy.

Since so much of our political interest had been centered on Trotsky and then later Stalin, and therefore about the USSR itself, I was surprised that James never went to Russia. I would surely have expected him to. It became easy enough to visit especially after the death of Stalin. With my own interest I went there four times: twice by ship to Leningrad, once by plane to Moscow, and once through the Mediterranean to Odessa.

After these travels I wrote a history of Russia titled, *The Russian Eagle,* a long book covering its origin and proceeding to the end of the Romanoff dynasty. My husband researched the Russian sources for me. It took me four and a half years to complete. I consider it one of my major achievements. My husband had said that what had first attracted him to me was my knowledge of all the Russian classics and my knowledge of its history.

I then wondered what James would have thought of the Soviet Union. I wonder now what James would think of what is happening in Russia today. While in all the western countries, Britain, France, Germany, Italy, the Communist Party is allowed and Communist members become mayors and members of Parliament, the Communist Party has been mostly dethroned in the whole of USSR, now Russia. The United States applauds the breakup of the Soviet Union, even though the U.S. northern states won the bloodiest war in its history to prevent the southern states from having a Confederation instead of a Union.

I have been to the Soviet Union enough times to feel that its people had become petit-bourgeoisie with a desire for more and more material goods. The East Germans had the same desire. They looked on their western counterpart and envied the greater affluence there. But soon they were shocked to find that 50,000 of them were suddenly unemployed. This situation was one they had never envisioned. Under the communist system, you were guaranteed a job, lodgings, however inadequate, free education, and free medicine.

In the United States, millionaires are two a penny. There are 100,000 multimillionaires, while there are millions of homeless and millions of North American children going to bed hungry.

The idea of communism was a common sharing. The people at the top might have fancy cars and dachas and country homes, but there were no vast differences in wealth. One has only to see the crowds in Moscow and elsewhere to notice they all seemed reasonably dressed and not at all ill-fed.

Under Stalin, though the social services remained the same, the people lived a life of fear under his terror. Trotsky's viewpoint, therefore, was that you had to get rid of the terror, not the system. Also, he felt that if there was an attack by capitalistic states against the USSR, it should be defended as still the first socialist nation; as he had helped defend it when Allied armies tried to overthrow the Soviets in 1918.

Then the Allies were supporting the White army and its Czarist generals, as today they are supporting the breakaway Republics and the reintroduction of the capitalist system.

James disagreed with those who supported the country while it was under the rule of Stalin. He had made no exception when making his few antiwar speeches. Again, I am surprised that James made no effort to go to Russia. After all, we had been closely concerned with what happened in that vast continent.

The evening that my woman friend prevented my meeting with James we were restricted to a long telephone talk. Probably, my friend thought we might have fallen into one of her beds. We might well have, but James had always been sure that we would meet again. We were both disappointed because we had been prevented from meeting and from having an evening alone together.

I talked to James and saw him only once more in our lifetime, though we had sporadic correspondence through the many years.

The next morning Barbara drove me to the halfway place where my sister's son picked me up in his car. The journey to my sister's was quite long, and we had devised it this way so that it would not be too tiring for Barbara or for my nephew. Barbara was quite cheerful all the way, and when I asked her why she had not given me James's telephone number earlier so we could have been together she said, "Oh I thought it was better that you did not." There was really nothing I could say to that, but I found it most peculiar. I then had a pleasant stay with my sister in Suffolk, but all the time I was waiting for a telegram from my husband. He had let me know that he was now well and would be taking a flight so that we could take the plane back to the States.

Home again, we settled down to our life on Long Island, going into New York to our respective offices each day, but enjoying our weekends in our house that overlooked the Sound and where we had a long stretch of beach which we could enjoy for walks over the weekends. My husband, too, had his hobby of gardening, and our garden was full of flowers and bushes, many hydrangeas in particular, and also silver birches, which is the Russian national tree.

Then one day, this was in the late sixties, I was reading the paper and found an advertisement that excited me. It stated James would be talking at one of the Long Island colleges. I told my husband we must go.

This must have been during James's second sojourn to the United States, which was from 1963 to 1980, with breaks in between. I cannot be exact about dates.

I sense that one of the happiest, or perhaps shall I say, serene times of James's life was when he was teaching at Howard University and Federal City University in Washington D.C., where they gave him an Honorary Doctors' Degree. He was also lecturing at other universities throughout the 1970's. He had been a teacher for several years in Trinidad before he left. He enjoyed teaching. This was one of the times he wrote to me and I felt a contentment in him with this new type of life he was leading. Here he could talk as much as he wanted. He had the attention and probably the devotion of his students. As a professor, he had respect. He had written me and sent me his address and telephone number as soon as he was settled. I still have it.

A younger brother of mine, who had known James in London, was living on Chesapeake Bay, where he had a house and huge garage, which he used as a studio. He was a documentary film maker.

I wrote him and gave him James's address and suggested he might invite him for a weekend. This he did, and James went to visit my brother and his wife. James did not seem to have said anything momentous and discussed politics very little during his stay. My brother showed him some of his ecological-social films. Evidently, James enjoyed them, sitting with a glass of whiskey in his hand. I had not known him to drink. In England we never celebrated with wine or any type of liquor.

James asked after me and sent me his love, as usual.

The evening my husband and I journeyed forth then to hear James, we did not really know the way to the college and we got lost, so that when we arrived, we were very late. We thought that we had missed the lecture altogether, however, when we finally found the room, while there was no one on the platform, there was James surrounded by a group of students. With a startled expression, he looked up and saw me, as if he could not believe his eyes. He said something to a young woman next to him and she came over to greet us. I think this may have been his third wife. She was very pleasant and stood and talked to us and said James would tear himself away from his students as soon as he could. I noticed him looking at me every few moments. The young woman mentioned that James had talked about me many times to her, and that he still remembered the first Socialist Social Dance where we had been together. She seemed to feel that it had been our first meeting, but of course our first meeting had been held at the dinner party at Doctor Hieger's house. So he had talked about me even to his third wife.

James came over to us with two hands outstretched and I put my two hands in his. He said, "Let us get away a little so we can talk." He took my hand and started leading me to the farther side of the room. His wife stayed where she was, but as James and I walked across the room, we realized that my husband was walking behind us, keeping us strictly in his sight. So that when we turned around and again clasped each other's hands and looked into each other's eyes, there was little that we could say with him standing there. I introduced the two men but our conversation was very limited. My husband seemed very suspicious of James and it made the encounter very awkward.

So, here were two abortive meetings we might have had, one in England and one in the States, years after we had been together. In one case my friend and in the other case my husband prevented us, so that we were not able to have any real rapport again. My husband soon took my arm, made our goodbyes to James and walked me to the door. I could feel James's eyes concentrated on my back. I decided it was better not to turn and look back at him again. It had been quite exciting to see him but it could have been so much a better meeting.

I never saw him again and only was in contact vicariously with him through my brother one time, and there was the continued occasional correspondence between us over the years.

We had both been going about our different lives over the many years. I cannot say that I thought of him often, only at times when I was reminded of him by letters. Oddly, my friend Barbara did occasionally, and I could almost sense a reluctance even in her letters, write about C. L. R. So from time to time, I was kept in touch with what was happening to him.

I had, over the years, various letters from Nello. I also received some from my first husband.

Except for ending usually with their love in both cases, they were not love letters. In both, I was told what was happening to them and about subjects which would interest me.

I would have liked to have had this continuing correspondence with both of them. I had shared a great deal with both. My new husband did not comment in any way about them, but I knew he was hurt. I wondered if I would be similarly upset if he was in correspondence with old lovers. I decided I probably would be. Also, I had no wish to hurt him. Therefore, I answered the letters, but briefly, unlike the way in which I would normally have responded, but I was pleased to receive them.

The letters stopped for a while. Then they would come again, and unwillingly I would have to reply in the same way.

At one time, I had a letter from James. The letter asked after me, my health and so on, and would I send him a copy of my latest book about which he had heard. I wondered how.

This was *The Spanish Caribbean,* a history of the development from Taino days to the present: or as the subtitle put it: From Columbus to Castro, of the three islands of Cuba, the Dominican Republic and Puerto Rico. I had spent a considerable amount of time on research for this book. It was published by G. K. Hall, in the University Series, in hard cover. It was afterwards reprinted, first in hard cover and then in soft cover, by Alfred Schenkman. This was the publisher of Ivor Oxaal's book on Trinidad.

In a preface, Ivor Oxaal wrote of C. L. R. James in glowing terms as a Renaissance Man. It was the first time I had seen it applied to him, as I have mentioned.

So Ivor Oxaal and I, for a while, had the same publisher, Alfred Schenkman. He was a very amiable intellectual. He had a Harvard degree, had acted as a minister for the Unitarian Fellowship of which Adlai Stevenson was a member, and finally become publisher of left wing books. He and I had an excellent relationship too and he would always publish anything I wrote. Unfortunately, he died after publishing four books of mine, three about the need for Puerto Rican independence.

Seeing the mention of C. L. R. in one of Oxaal's books brought back memories of James that I had almost forgotten.

Ivor Oxaal called Schenkman "the best publisher I ever had." His book was *Race and Revolutionary Consciousness: A Report on the 1970 Black Power Revolt in Trinidad.*

The book on Trinidad also reminded me of James. I wondered why he had not been there at that crucial time in his native land. The crowds held banners aloft praising the names of many American negroes, but not C. L. R. James.

Earlier, I had written a book about the love affair of a black man and a white woman. I made the circumstances, the stage, as it were, different from that which had existed between Nello and myself. Still a great deal of what I wrote naturally came from my experience with him. The crisis in the book was the necessity of the woman to have an abortion.

After the letter from him, I sent him a copy of the book he wanted, and perhaps with a sense of mischief, sent him the novel too. Perhaps he was upset by it. Probably because I had made it a love affair between a black man and a white woman, which our relationship had never been. Color was not a factor.

James said there had been few books on the relationship of black men and white women. Here I had written one called *Lirazel*.

I understood he told someone that the sexual side of our relationship had been more important to me than him. I am sure this was not so. He continued that I was not a woman for half measures, and that this realization made me break up our love affair.

This again was not so.

Desire for each other had been mutual. In London the color question too had never arisen.

But he did not reply for a long time and I thought he was offended by *Lirazel*.

I believe James knew little of the Puerto Rican struggle for independence. He wrote to me this time both through my publisher and through a mutual friend, Professor Gordon Lewis. Gordon had a Trinidadian wife, Sybil, who knew James and his family at home. When I first came to Puerto Rico, I met them both and our mutual friendship of James became a common bond. Though C. L. R. in two of his letters told me he did not like Gordon. Gordon had a sharp wit, probably Nello had felt the bite of his tongue in some earlier encounters.

Gordon Lewis's most famous and authoritative book was *Puerto Rico: Freedom And Power In The Caribbean*. He was not only a professor of Social Sciences at the University of Puerto Rico but became Director of the Institute of Caribbean Studies. He was also a consultant to the government of Trinidad and Tabago and the U.S. Virgin Islands, and the University of Guyana. He was also visiting professor at the University of Chicago, California at Los Angeles, Harvard University and of Oxford University in England. He had helped write Puerto Rico's Constitution in 1952.

So I had met up again with a stimulating intellectual friend for some years, whose passion was politics. He was not, however, a Marxist, but a socialist of Fabian style. We discussed world and Caribbean politics almost exclusively.

His wife knew James well, so the three of us would often discuss him. I told them frankly what our relationship had been. They were interested. They themselves had a white/black relationship, and their children were varying shades of color. They lived in a big old house and had frequent parties. For a time I was able to go to them and met a highly diverse group of university professors and visitors from different countries.

They came too with their children to our house and Gordon and I tended to be left alone to talk about all the subjects of our mutual interest. He too was an "independentista."

I did not keep Nello's letters because of my husband's unease about James. But this letter was found amongst James' letters after he died. It was the only one he ever typed to me, the others he wrote in his own hand even though the writing became quavering as time passed.

May 16, 1977

L. L. Cripps
JJ-38 Dorado del Mar
Dorado, Puerto Rico
My Dear Lillian,

Do not misjudge me and my deep continuing regard for you because I have not made any response to the book you have sent to me. It is an excellent piece of work with some very solid research behind it. However, I was away in England for a year which made a complete mess of my correspondence. All I can do now is to send you this letter C/O Schenkman Publishing Co.

I am also going to send you a copy of the letter C/O Gordon K. Lewis. He is no friend of mine but I am not going to put my name outside so he may send it on to you. At any rate my dear Lillian, let me hear from you. Your book reminds me not only of what you call "past labors" but "past good and valuable times."

As ever,
(signed) Nello
C. L. R. James

P.S.
My hand gives me a lot of trouble and therefore I write as little as possible.

The book referred to is *The Spanish Caribbean*.

The letter was written forty years after we parted but shows he still felt warmly about me and had kept a very kind remembrance of me over the many years.

And his "deep continuing regard." He had always remembered me.

James was obviously circumspect in this letter since this was sent after he had met my second husband on Long Island.

Perhaps I should explain the 'Lilian.' My two names are Lilian Louise. I was still using my first name when I knew James. But my first husband had a sister called Lilian, so we both had the same name. After a while, I decided to start using my second name Louise, to avoid the confusion, and from then on kept to that. In his letter I noticed Nello never mentioned the novel I had sent him, only praised the *Spanish Caribbean* book. His phrase "past good and valuable times" was surely to remind me of our long ago love affair.

I thought his comment on my book, "It is an excellent piece of work with some solid research behind it", was a little sparse since he had asked me to send him the book. It was like a teacher marking a student's term paper.

And he never mentioned a word about the novel that dealt with a black and white relationship.

Part Three
Looking Back

11
Looking Back

FOR JAMES, I THINK THAT THE TIME HE SPENT IN THE JOHNSON-Forest group was a time spent "in the wilderness," which is how his admiring biographer Paul Buhle describes it. His going to England originally had been good. He had established himself as a writer. *The Life of Captain Cipriani, Minty Alley, The Black Jacobins, World Revolution* were published. He had had the necessary political indoctrination in our group, and the necessary political experience in the ILP. He could have gone to the United States and seen the conditions there for blacks. He could have met Trotsky and produced his long article on *The Negro Question* in the United States.

He was then forty. It was time for him to go home to Trinidad. We could have married and gone together. He could have easily obtained a position as a teacher again and become self-supporting. He had helped bring out a political periodical. He was all ready to begin the political activity by which he could have formed his party and which would have made him prime minister of Trinidad and a leader in the Caribbean. He had still half a lifetime before him. I might have gone with him to help in the editing of a journal and written my own books on the Caribbean.

But on second thought, I believe it would have been best if he had returned to his first wife. He still spoke tenderly of her. He would have been gone eight years. Or he could have found a new wife, a fellow woman compatriot.

I write this because his third wife, Selma Weinstein, did go with him when he belatedly returned to his island. She worked hard with him in bringing out *The Nation,* Eric Williams's party paper, one that should have been James's. Evidently, the third marriage was a mistake for "both sides." George Lamming has written a book based on the tumultuous relationship of the marriage. Instead of that obvious part that would, I believe, have given James the true stature of which he was capable, he digressed.

James's last work was his cricket book. He could still have written a good book on the subjects but the philosophical discourses would instead have been substituted with political forecasting and wisdom of his region and the world.

Since I have been writing this book, I think of how I would have liked James to use his many talents. Though even if I had been his wife those many years ago, I am sure I would not have changed him from his chosen path. Yet I think of how much greater influence he could have been in the sphere that I would have chosen for him. Only since I have lived in the Caribbean have I had this vision. It was not apparent to me when I lived in England. If he had gone earlier, he could not only have been the leader in his island, but also a leader in the Caribbean. He could have had a voice in the United Nations. His name would have been known to millions, especially millions of blacks. He still could have written his books. He could have led his countrymen down the path of socialism in which he believed if he had gone back to his roots and worked there during his long life. Visits to Africa, the United States, England, and other Caribbean islands would still have been part of his life. He could have received world recognition and his name known to black masses everywhere.

His leadership of a black movement in the United States was never a realistic goal. James achieved a great deal in various fields in his lifetime, but he wandered in different directions. He completely changed his political perspective three times, breaking away from Trotskyism, then Leninism, then Marxism.

My view now, after having lived in the Caribbean for twenty years, is that he could and should have been a tremendous leader in the Caribbean. In fact, I realize that if he had been prepared in the forties to work in Trinidad, I could have gone with him, and there it would have been possible for us to have lived together.

Speaking at the Caribbean Unity Conference in 1973, James spoke about the revolution that happened in Trinidad just previously, which was symptomatic, he said, of what was happening in the Caribbean. Despite the recent happening in Trinidad, he talks of the extreme revolutionary backwardness in the Caribbean. He says that he talked to a group of West Indian intellectuals, and told them: "'Here you are all babbling about this and that and you are not getting ready for the thing you are.' They looked at me and they were somewhat bewildered. The world believed that they were. He told them when the situation broke in Trinidad, then later in Guyana, they should have been prepared for it."

If they should have been prepared for it, he should have been prepared for it. Why was he not in the Caribbean at that time? Why was he not in Trinidad? Why was he not in Guyana? He says: "You do not wait until the revolution takes place. You prepare for it in advance." He did not prepare for it; he was not even in the West Indies where he should have been when it took place.

He goes on to say: "What happened in Trinidad is no surprise to me. I would have been ready for it." If he had been ready for it, why was he not there? He further goes on: "What are you all doing. You are just talking and talking about the revolution and what you are going to do but you are doing nothing. The question that matters is the seizure of power and that is what you have to be prepared for." He never prepared for it.

That is what I would have wished him to have done; to have been there in his native area preparing for the revolutionary movements that were to take place there, instead of having discussions with a group of admiring women, writing pamphlets, and begging not to be deported from the United States. He told his audience about a group of four who went to a bank and got hold of two hundred thousand dollars. He was highly indignant because they went back home and went to sleep, and later the police came and arrested them and got a large part of the money. He says: "I cannot get over it."

I am laughing as I write this because I imagine his astonishment at someone getting hold of two hundred thousand dollars and then waiting for the police to come. He said: "You put your hands on two hundred thousand out of a bank and then half an hour after the money that should have been perhaps going to Barbados or somewhere to be put aside, or something else should have been done with it." He does not say exactly what should have been done with it.

I wonder what he would have said about the *macheteros* who actually got hold of seven-and a half million dollars in Connecticut and got away with it.* Unfortunately, they claimed they were the ones who did the bombing. They got some publicity, but a number of them went to prison, so they spent a great deal of money on lawyers, and they did give out Christmas presents to some children in Connecticut. They should not have claimed the bank robbery but let the police find them and catch them. The police never recovered the money. They themselves must have used some of it, and,

---

*The *macheteros* are a group of Puerto Rican *independentistas,* mostly intellectuals, lawyers, artists, writers, teachers. They have suffered grievously for proclaiming their guilt with long terms in United States prisons.

in fact, used some of their own money and mortgaged some money of their relatives by their proclamation of guilt.

What James's attitude would have been I do not know, but I guess he would have been even more astounded that people could get hold of money successfully, whisk it away, and then stand up and say, "We did it."

James tells these young Caribbean men and women in 1973 that: "There is an incurable cross that exists in the masses of the population in all governments and opposition in the Caribbean today." This is my whole theory of what James should have been doing with his life. That he should have been getting ready for the tumult that would take place in the various Caribbean islands. He might have helped to save Grenada from a U.S. invasion.

Apart from his political paths, there are other sectors of his life that I do not view well. Looking back, I find myself unsympathetic about his attitude toward money. He was ready for others to support him financially. This is neither a puritan attitude nor one that conformed to the public school code nor the wider general British code of "what is done." So though he writes that he subscribes to both these codes, his actual life belies this. He had three wives, a love affair with me, and numerous other relationships with women. I do not think that the Puritans would have approved.

In regards to financial matters, this started from the beginning in Trinidad, in 1930. Before he left, he told Learie Constantine, who was visiting Trinidad, that he was planning to go to England and write, but he lacked the money. Constantine replied: "You come to England, do your writing, and if things get tough I will see you through."

James said: "I accept the offer."

Constantine not only supported James while he lived with him in Lancashire, but also continued to send him money, from time to time, when he was in London forming our group. James went to see his old friend to say good-bye before he left for the United States. Constantine completely outfitted James with new clothes for the adventure and also gave him an expensive camera as a going away gift.

Again, in regards to money, in a letter to Trotsky, in 1939, while he was still being supported by the SWP, James suggested that he should initiate a new organization of Negroes: a suggestion made by Trotsky. James sets up the program, writing: "The aim must be to bring the masses in though not with Marcus Garvey with his wild 'Back to Africa' schemes." This is rather rough when he had worked with Mrs. Garvey for a while in London, and surely here he is taking a harsh position in regards to her ex-husband. He goes on to add: "The political tension today is infinitely higher than in Garvey's time and they will follow a movement which looks as if it needs to do something, and is not proposed by feeble groups of intellectuals." He continues: "Our party is important."

Then he writes that his health is not good, that he needs to rest. While resting, he will write a book about seventy-five thousand words long, about the U.S. Negro situation. Lastly, he says he needs five hundred dollars advance on the book, especially since he has, "certain financial obligations to meet in Great Britain."

This is a begging letter. The new black organization was never started. James said, regarding the audience for his proposed book, "It surely has many thousands." Was he not sufficiently motivated to write the book, even though he did not get financial help? Many artists create their paintings, writers write their books, when they have financial situations that are low and insecure. When James wrote that letter, he was still being supported by the members of the SWP. He allowed Freddie Paine and her husband to support him and to pay for the printing and distribution of his and their political efforts.

When he worked in Trinidad, he was paid for his work as editor of *The Nation* by Eric Williams's People's National Movement (PNM). He was also supported by some funds from the Oilfield Workers' Trade Unions. When later he wished to return to Trinidad, he asked that a public subscription should be raised for that purpose. The offer was never taken up, and it was really quite an astounding and arrogant statement for him to have made.

James respected what he called the sterling "English character." He had applied this term to a businessman he had known in Nelson, Lancashire, when he first came to England. These were characteristics of the English that he had been brought up to believe, while growing up in Trinidad. A man does not act like a cad or a bounder. Especially he had found this to be so on the cricket field.

These characteristics were generally true in the British population, from the highest to the lowest, a fundamental honesty. This was so at least in my time. Whether there have been changes in the ensuing half century is likely. They have been everywhere else. Accepting money to support oneself did not fit into the "sterling British character" he admired.

Looking back, I would rather remember the young James I loved, so delightful to the eye, so full of talent, so full of promise, so ready to go out and set the wrongs of the world to right, rather than the middle-aged man asking for money or the old man puffing vaingloriously about his achievements.

But I smile in remembrance of him with great fondness. Yet why, when he was young and had all the world before him, did neither he nor I think of his going back to the West Indies to be a leader? He helped others later, such as Nkrumah, to be an African leader, and he was ready to help others. Why did he not think of where his own roots lay? It would have been so natural a step. Why was he so entranced by the United States, wanting to stay there?

The idea of Trinidad did later arise, but it was then too late. Why did I not think of it? But I did not understand or have much knowledge then except for the affairs that were occupying our small group. Now, looking back, it seems so natural a path for him to have taken, at a time and place when his full talents would have blossomed. His move into the Johnson/Forest Tendency now seems to me such a small backwater for him to have passed so many years.

For myself, I make no apology for working for British and French Relief. I had no bad conscience about it. I was helping those hurt by war. When I was confronted with a choice of three marriages, my life would have been different if I had chosen to have gone back to my husband. At first, he had found it difficult to earn sufficient money to continue as a literary writer. Then I would have had to continue working with my magazines. When he became successful, of course, my life would have changed, and I could have started again to write. Though he traveled around the world a couple of times, interviewing specialists and writing about cancer and heart disease, he then settled in New York, writing popular novels.

It would have meant I probably would never have come to Puerto Rico. The last twenty years I have lived here would never have happened. I would never have found a new cause as I had in London with Nello. I would gladly have given up my years in the States to work again harmoniously with him in the cause for Trinidad's and the Caribbean's independence.

Looking back, I remember Nello with affection, sometimes with a slight amusement, as he evades questions put to him, in his later years. Then, with admiration for his many talents; for certain of his writings that had been so good; of our relationship. It was an exciting, fulfilling one to have had in youth. But let me say again, I was never his disciple. I have known several men in my long life other than James who had finer minds than James had. I had already mentioned Adlai Stevenson and Bertrand Russell. A tender memory I have of Bertrand Russell is his putting his hands around a china teacup to warm them. Now I had been brought up in a society that one did not do this. But here I was in high society with an "Earl of the Realm." Here he was putting his two hands around the teacup. I think of his general philosophies in those weekends I spent at his home, I learned one chooses those social graces and precepts as are relevant to oneself.

Then there was Havelock Ellis. We used to go to the house of writer Hugh de Selincourt for weekends. His wife was a pianist and his daughter a cellist. Striding over on a Sunday morning, Havelock Ellis would come dressed in a Sherlock Holmes-style long coat and cape, and we would talk all morning and listen to music. We talked on every possible subject and before lunch would have a dry sherry. I was therefore well acquainted with him.

And of course, we discussed sex about which Havelock Ellis had written five authoritative books. I did not know then but learned later that when Marie Stopes came to England on visits, she became the lover of both men.

Another friend I include is Roger Baldwin. He was the founder of the American Civil Liberties Union and, later, was their counsel in the United Nations. In this way he became familiar with all the heads of state and certainly with all the ambassadors around the world. He had, as a young man, like Bertrand Russell, gone to prison because of his antiwar activities. He had been, as a young man, a friend of my sister-in-law because she was dating his roommate at Harvard. This was a long-standing friendship. When we were in Puerto Rice, he used to stay through the winter, and he would always come to see us. He had a fund of knowledge, and we had a quantity of good conversations and discussions with him over the years. He had, when he was young, visited with Prince Kropotkin. This was of great interest to my Russian husband, even though his politics were far removed from that of an anarchist. Roger Baldwin, when I sent him my manuscript of *The Spanish Caribbean,* passed it on to the New York Public Library to store in their archives. He died in his nineties but was alert until his last winter, unable to make the journey back to the island.

I would also put Professor Gordon Lewis on a level with James. I have already mentioned why I would do this in another chapter. He attended Balliol College, Oxford University, and then Harvard. And James had only a colonial secondary school education. This does make a difference. Gordon was also sharper in his mind, much more logical than James was. He wrote, too, better prose.

My Zionist friend should also be included. He was Oxford and Harvard trained and one of Felix Frankfurter's bright young lawyers. He was with Ben-Gurion at the signing of the treaty that made

Israel a country, and he sat at the roundtable with Lord Balfour and was received by King George V.

I also would suggest other men who had talents as high as James's. For instance, there was Norman Thomas. I used to travel on the Long Island Railroad, which was an hour's journey, every week over a considerable period. He also came to talk to my group when I was working for Adlai Stevenson. When he was dying in a local hospital I was asked to go and read to him *The New York Times,* which we had shared together on our commuting trains. I did not do so. I could not bear to see him dying and I am not good in a sick room.

In a different field, but equally prominent, was Dr. Paul Dudley White, my cardiologist.

My husband's father was an internationally known physiologist. During Lenin's time he was allowed out, on several occasions, not only to the States but to various conferences in Europe. He went to Harvard to give several months of teaching. While he was there his two sons, my husband and his twin brother, were students at Harvard. My husband also later lectured at Harvard. But while there, Dr. White and my husband's father met and became good friends so that when I had my first heart attack, he became my cardiologist. He was at the same time the cardiologist for President Eisenhower.

We used to then travel up, quite frequently, to Boston and its environs to see my brother-in-law and also to see my publisher, Alfred Shenckman—who perhaps should also be included in this list and was himself a Harvard man—and to see Dr. Paul Dudley White. We not only saw Dr. White in his office, but we always went either over to his house in Belmont or else we went out to dinner at a Greek restaurant near the Bay that was a favorite of his. He was then not only interested in heart disease but far wider fields. I believe he was the only North American to be made a member of the Soviet Scientific Community. I forget its exact name. He was also put up as a candidate for the Nobel Peace Prize, though he did not receive it. It was Dr. White who suggested that my husband and I should come down to Puerto Rico because he said if we did so, it would at least extend our lives ten years. It did in fact extend our lives ten years. I had heart disease and my husband had emphysema. Dr. White was also quite well known in Puerto Rico because he was the doctor of Pablo Casals, the famous cellist, and he knew various members of the government. He recommended a doctor for me when we retired.

Another doctor in this category was Dr. Benjamin Spock. He used to be my son's doctor long before he became famous. He would climb the four flights to our apartment. Alone with my son, I naturally was nervous whenever he had even a slight temperature, and Dr. Spock would always stay a while to help me relax. He did not like Mickey Mouse, for some reason, and he would make funny imitations of Mickey Mouse to amuse my son and me. He also talked to me about his theories on bringing up children. He told me one story, I remember, about how his son, I think then about eight, did not want to tie his shoelaces when they were going out to visit some friends. He argued with the boy for a little while, and then he said to himself: "Well why not let the boy do it? I will be beside him to see that he is not in any danger, but he will find out that he will fall over on those loose laces and I will have made my point in a practical way without having to argue with him." He said this was done and the boy did fall over his laces and then sheepishly tied them up.

I think from Bertrand Russell and from Dr. Spock, I developed my ideas on the education and the upbringing of children that I wrote about in the long years of publishing and editing my magazines for parents.

Another man that I put in the same category with James, at least as an equal, but again, in a different field, was George Grosz, the famous caricaturist and artist, and strong anti-Hitlerian. We had some friends nearby who were artists, and George Grosz used to visit them fairly often. Glass in hand—he always liked a glass in hand—I would sit and talk to him, often for a long time, or a group of us would sit and discuss; but more generally, I think of the times when he and I would discuss the world and its many problems.

I have mentioned Stevenson only briefly. What happened was this:

I remember walking along Fifty-ninth Street and Fifth Avenue with a friend, when coming toward us, a few yards away, was Adlai Stevenson with a companion. As we approached each other, I said: "Good morning, Mr. Stevenson." He turned toward me after our friends each took a step or two away. I told him I was Chairwoman for Suffolk County on his behalf. We stopped and chatted for a few moments, and he asked how the campaign was faring in our area.

Some weeks later I received an invitation to meet with him and a few others at the St. Regis Hotel. At one point we stood together to have a photograph taken. When that was over, I said: "Do you remember me? I accosted you in the streets, a short time ago." He looked very startled, eyebrows up, and looked at me more intently. I realized I had used the word that is almost used exclusively in a context with prostitutes in the United States. We use it in a much wider context in England.

I think from the moment I used that word, he showed interest in me. We stood and talked together. I told him of the discussion group, in his name, that I had formed, and of our work in Suffolk County. He asked that I write him and keep him informed. When I sent him a letter he would answer in his own handwriting and sign "that man."

I also knew John Dewey. He was the schoolboard director of my child's progressive school. There were only eighty students, and my son stayed there from the age of two until he was eight years old. During those six years John Dewey usually appeared at the parents' meetings. Naturally, we talked about the children and about education in general. I had heard, of course, of the Dewey Commission for the Defense of Trotsky when I was in London and working with James's Trotskyist group.

Somehow I never realized that this director of the school was the same man who had headed that other organization. How I wish I had. What a great pleasure it would have been to talk to him about Trotsky. I also had not realized that he was a good friend of Bertrand Russell. Indeed, he was the one who had obtained for Russell his position with the Barnes Foundation, when Russell was being hounded about a possible professorship at New York University. Again I would have loved to have talked to Dewey about Russell. But the subject never came up. Also, when I had seen Russell, while we had talked of many things, such as how his children were adjusting to the United States and his young new wife and how they were settling down, Dewey's name never arose.

I suppose there was no reason that it should have, but I wish I had known. It would have been another source of pleasure to talk to this man of stature about another man I had known. As Lady Ottoline Morrell said: "Bertrand Russell was a man of awesome intellect.'" I agreed.

I remember, too, in my university days, a number of professors who influenced me and who I consider as being equal in stature to James. I went around London University attending lectures I thought might be interesting. I listened to the brilliant Malinovski, and I have continued the interest in anthropology that began with him. Even today I receive the glossy quarterly *Cultural Survival* written by United States anthropologists from prestigious universities, whose articles cover the problems of native peoples all over the world.

Then, there was Harold Laski, Labor Party MP, who used to

invite a few students to his home for tea on Sundays and who taught the realities of politics. There was G. B. Harrison, Shakespearean scholar, who later moved to the University of Chicago, who used to take two or three of us to tea at a well-known tea shop. I always spooned the cream of a Charlotte Russe while we batted about ideas.

Most of all, there was Jack Isaacs, unknown except to his many students who packed his lectures. He would take a few of us to art galleries and show us how to look at paintings in a new way and to notice how the paint was applied to the canvasses to achieve effects. He brought poets and writers for a few of us to hear. I well remember Edith Sitwell, thin, gowned in a high-necked, full-length dress of green, and wearing a long chain with a large piece of exotic jewelry between her narrow breasts. I had a special relationship with him. He would invite me to his flat. He took me to the Cafe Royale, the meeting place for Oscar Wilde and the *fin de siecle* poets and artists. He also took me to Rules, which the modern artists and writers frequented. I remembered the first time I danced with him, and he asked me as we danced around the floor whether I was a virgin. I told him I was. He still pursued me to my youthful and mischievous delight.

I knew, though not well, Austrian Professor Leopold Kohr, now 82, and his titled British wife, when they moved in the academic circles of the University of Puerto Rico and went to small gatherings where he lectured on his theory of "Small Is Beautiful." He has recently been named by the *Sunday Times of London,* as one of the thousand "makers of the 20th century." "Kohr is an innovator of genius," the newspaper stated. He has also now been called "a prophet and a genius," by others, as James has been. At one time, with the support of the government and that of a few wealthy backers, he was asked to put his ideas into practice on the tiny Caribbean island of Anguilla, which then declared itself independent. I remember the advertisements he and his supporters placed in the *New York Sunday Times.*

"We Are Not A Nation Of Busboys": meaning, they did not want to have their lives dedicated to a place "for fun in the sun" just for tourists. His thesis is that cities should be just large enough to be able to support the arts, music, opera, theater, but no larger; that countries should be small enough, so the people would know all about those that governed them, and they should be small enough sovereign states of unions of people with different historic roots. He wrote a number of books on the subject. With the breakup of Eastern Europe and the USSR, he has now achieved some fame for his theories.

I met the well-known scientist Theodosius Dobzhansky many times at the home of Yugoslavian Milislav Demeretz, friend of my second husband, who at that time headed the Carnegie Institute in Cold Spring Harbor, Long Island. We lived nearby and were invited to social scientific gatherings and small dinner parties. These occasions were pleasant for my second husband. Science is a field of which I have no knowledge, but a few of us would sit on the balcony of the house overlooking Long Island Sound; then the talk would range into the areas of philosophy in which I could enter. Once or twice I met Dr. James Watson there, codiscoverer of the double helix. And when I was already in Puerto Rico Mrs. Dobzhansky, herself a brilliant woman, came to stay with me for several weeks, while our husbands were off on other ventures.

I thought of C. L. R. James then as a brilliant man of many talents, especially a great conversationalist, an exceptional orator, a great reader and writer of importance, a friendly, lovable man, but I never thought of him as an intellectual.

So after a long life, I have known a fairly large number of men with whom I can measure James intellectually. He was talented. He had many gifts. He was in many ways different from them. They all worked in different fields. It was not that he was black and they were white. Color did not enter into the equation. Nor was it that they were friends and he was my lover. I had matured, so I could withhold only in some ways the admiration that many latecomers gave him. But my love and long friendship with him still hold.

12

James and Women

WHAT WAS JAMES'S ATTITUDE TOWARD WOMEN?

I know only what they were toward me. He had three wives. He had other "affairs" too. There was his public stance on the subject, which was the correct liberal one of equality.

Though he made the correct statements of belief on the equality of the sexes on the platform, he evidently found it difficult to follow personally.

James wrote an excellent forty-four page essay titled "The Atlantic Slave Trade and Slavery," which was first published in *Amistad*, in 1970, in a collection of works by Negro writers on black history and literature. It was later published in his collected works.

In it, he has one paragraph in which he equates women's rights and black rights and makes reference to marriage.

The Abolitionists "fought for the emancipation of women."

He wrote:

> Oberlin College, the first college to accept Negroes in the United States, was also the first college to accept women in the United States, becoming the first co-educational institution of higher learning.

Then, "what Margaret Fuller and other great female abolitionists were trying to establish was their right to establish relationships with men in which they were not in effect the chattels of their husbands through the marriage contract."

These words seem to indicate that he did not believe marriage necessary for a good relationship between a man and a woman.

However, despite this statement of equality, from my experience I know that in any relationship, James still felt the man needed to be the dominant partner. Actually, this attitude extended beyond women. In any group of men and women, he wanted to be the leader. And men and women gave him that right. So it was not just the man/woman relationship. He had those qualities for which others allowed him the dominant role. I say this affectionately, but he was in many ways a very arrogant and self-glorifying man. He wrote of the West Indian Negroes' "magnificent virility." And he obviously included himself. He was not modest.

He was young when I knew him. I was about twenty-seven and he was about thirty-one, a good age difference between a man and a woman. He was mostly serious but would often laugh. I had some excellent photographs of him with his head thrown back and laughing. Unfortunately, I lost the photographs.

He said he had had to subdue his natural gaiety in England.

It seems too that he lost some of that gaiety as he grew older. He also looked for much younger women than himself. The difference between James and his first American wife was twenty years. The difference between his age and his second wife was thirty years.

About black men and white women, in an article on the West Indies, James wrote:

"Fair skinned girls who marry dark men are often ostracized by their families and given up as lost. There have been cases of fair women who have been content to live with black men but not marry them."

He was writing of conditions in the West Indies in the 1930's, soon after he had left Trinidad.

I wonder if the bigotry of racism in the United States ever affected his wives. I was never aware of it in London. But in New York it would have been different. Recently I came across the following, which gives a further slant.

In the New York Times Book Review of August, 1992, a black woman novelist Bebe Moore Campbell recounts this story. She and three other black "sisters" are dining together in a restaurant when a handsome, well-known black man enters. His companion is a white woman. She and her friends are angry: obsessionally angry.

"Almost every time I get together with two or more African-American women, the topic turns to the problem. We're disgusted; we're depressed. We're obsessing."

"Yes, I want my people to date and marry each other and I don't think it will ever give me pleasure to see black men with white women."

Did James encounter this antagonism when he went about with white women? I wonder. There were also as well as his wives, the white women in the Johnson/Forest group he must have escorted in public.

In regard to children, James wrote: "A baby means, in modern civilisation, three years or more out of a woman's life.... For an active woman is posed the question, the home versus the career."

This is not so for the educated woman with a career. She can work far into her pregnancy, as I did. This is perfectly viable in today's workplace. A woman can also, if she is earning a reasonable salary, get someone to look after the baby at home, and she need not be tied down. I worked for many years and still looked after my baby without the help of a father. My child was certainly not neglected. I gave him a tremendous amount of love and devotion.

James also wrote:

> The man and his wife may both work but almost inevitably, the responsibilities of the home fall upon the woman, not only in the material sense of cooking and cleaning but in the sense that, except in rare cases, the responsibility for adjustments to differences in personality fall almost automatically upon her.

If a woman has work that pays reasonably well, it is possible for someone not only to look after her baby, but also to help her with the cleaning and cooking. Obviously James's opinion about a woman's making the adjustments to differences in personality is personal. For him, a baby is almost an impediment to a relationship between a man and a woman. I found that out. He also did not want me to go out and earn a living, so that we could have the baby and a small apartment. I imagine that this was also the case with his other women.

James married his first wife, Juanita, in 1930. Two years later, he left her to go to England alone. Some two years later, we became lovers. There had been other women in between, I learned, but none with whom he had had more than a few months' relationship. When our affair started, he told Gupta that this one was different from anything else he had previously felt. Our daily companionship spread over five years, and our liason lasted roughly three years.

But I think that James acted in his own interest without regard for his wife, even though he talked of her tenderly after leaving her. Despite his speech making and writing about women's rights, in fact, he acted differently, it seems, in his private life. He did not treat women in the way he spoke of them in public.

He left his first wife in Trinidad because he did not think she could fit into the life he had mapped out for himself.

Constance Webb, his second wife, wrote poetically of him.

> His . . . neck curved forward like that of a racehorse in the slip. . . . But as with highly trained athletes the tension was concentrated and timed, so that he gave the impression of enormous ease . . . the impact of his

first sentence was astounding.... He was our captive and we were a captivated audience.

Constance Webb imagines him a racehorse. I remember an idiosyncrasy of James. He would breathe in deeply, then let out a great snort rather like that of a thorobred horse.

I think he was a great orator: The "born talker" had become the most able of public speakers.

I believe he was irked by any harness put upon him by marriage. Marriage needs adjustments in day-to-day living by both partners. He did not want any restraints.

So it seems it was the same with his future wives. Constance Webb wanted to be treated as an equal, and her desires put on the same footing as the political demands made on him.

He acted, in the period of wooing her, as a teacher. He wrote long letters to her about art and literature, and he undoubtedly enjoyed that role.

He had a young son by her, but the responsibility for the child remained with his mother. His son had been sacrificed to James's political life, as I had realized my son would have been if I had succumbed and had married him in New York. Luckily, I had recognized the danger. Evidently, James's son in later life became, sadly, a drifter, possibly because his father had not been ready to accept full responsibility for him or because his father did not see him often.

James and Constance Webb were married in 1950, and by 1952 he was deported.

The boy's name was Nobby. At some later stage, James took him to Trinidad and said he was a "true James." But the boy did not see his father very often, and Constance Webb had the difficulty of bringing up a child on her own. It could not have been easy for her.

For some reason after his long wooing of her and before they got married, he had difficulties in obtaining a divorce from his first wife. I do not understand why. I had obtained my divorce just by going to Arkansas for a weekend. When we had discussed marriage in London and in New York, he had said his wife Juanita was ready to give him one.

His marriage to Constance Webb fell apart soon after it took place. He had said that it was made not only out of his own love, but also as a token of his designed Americanization.

James was evidently not capable of staying within the limits imposed by marriage.

Our love affair was outside those bounds, so he enjoyed it without any ties, only our desires. Yet with other love affairs later he felt constricted, and probably more constricted as a husband, since all his marriages were filled with friction.

James was handsome and proud. One time I said, "He had the pride of a peacock and the litheness of a leopard." Despite the frequent laughter we enjoyed together, he was a serious man. He was also, what he hoped to be, that is, a gentle man, in all respects: courteous, kind, and considerate. But he was vain even when I knew him, and I believe he grew more vain over time. His followers in the end, turned him into a prodigy.

I did not think of him like that. I thought of my love as the most interesting companion of my life. With me he certainly was a very gentle man and as wonderful a lover as any woman could wish.

But I was never a disciple. In particular, women would swoon over him. Esther Hieger was when she had enticed me to go to Paris when James was there. She was only one of many who succumbed to his charm, his charisma, over the years. His charm was particularly apparent when he was speaking on a platform. I think his being black increased women admirers' curiosity about him.

Constance Webb left him; I left him; and later Selma Weinstein, his third wife left him.

Raya Dunayevskaya is said in the end, to have broken with James in the Johnson/Forest group because she did not think he was treating her as an equal.

Women with whom James worked daily were all highly intelligent women and mostly good-looking; James only wanted beautiful women, Constance Webb had been a starlet and, therefore, was a good-looking woman. Around him, at the time, was Grace Lee—maybe she reminded him of his first wife, who was half Chinese. She later married James Boggs, who wrote *Pages from a Negro Worker's Notebook,* a dynamic statement from a black workingman who was also an intellectual and an excellent writer. She had perhaps found another man like James.

When James and I discussed books or analyzed political situations, we did so as equals. He was a great lover. And he told me I was the best lover he had ever known. That, of course, was when he was still a young man in his early thirties. Whether he met a better lover later, I do not know. But he still remembered me to the end of his life.

As he said: "We came together as two human beings made for each other."

Looking back I wonder: If we had married would it have lasted? His three marriages did not. I doubt mine with him would have done. Except in one circumstance of which I have only thought of recently, that is of our going together to Trinidad.

This book has a fair amount of autobiography which I felt was necessary, because James's women were and what they were like tells about an important factor: his own character. It would be good to have the autobiographies of the three other women who spent five years or more with C. L. R.: Constance Webb, whom he wooed for so long, and who gave him a son; his North American second wife Selma Weinstein, who married him in England and went with him to Trinidad to help him edit the periodical *The Nation,* and Raya Dunayevskaya, who had been a secretary to Trotsky for a short time, and who worked jointly with C. L. R. to form the Johnson/Forest Tendency. These books about themselves and their relationship with James would give great depths in portraying the manner of man that he was.

James suggests that women are brought up "in the art of catching a man, in the art of keeping him, using feminine wiles and tricks centuries old. This at the same time that her mind and direction are turned to revolt against any attempt to inhibit or curb her equality, or to force her into a feminine mold." It is therefore not only between herself and her man, there is a clash, but clashes inside herself are reflections of the two societies into which she is formed."

This is a male chauvinist statement. Certainly I had used no tricks or wiles with him. Perhaps he perceived this only in a marriage. I can only think, in looking back, that because we had no adjustments to make as in marriage, that our love remained good.

I never was out to catch him or any other man. I did not use any feminine wiles, "centuries old," to trick any man I knew. I certainly was not in revolt against any attempt to inhibit or curb my equality because no man that I knew or had had any relation with had ever attempted to curb it. Certainly, between James and me there was never any such clash. I made no attempt to catch him, or to keep him. In fact, when the time came, I was the one to walk away.

James's third wife, Selma Weinstein, was thirty years his junior. Their marriage went wrong early. Yet she perhaps filled the role of a "Krupskaya," better than his previous women. She went with him and they married in England in 1956, but it ended in 1982. It was his longest alliance. She was an avid feminist and thus must have acted outside her given role. She herself became a leader in the women's movement in the United States after she and James separated. Though there was never a divorce, they separated. When they went to Trinidad, she worked hard with him on editing *The Nation.*

His last marriage, evidently a stormy one, became the material for a novel by George Lamming.

George Lamming was one of the West Indians who gathered around James when he returned to England in 1953.

James had written about me in one of his long letters to Constance Webb before their marriage, telling her how much he missed me. I do not understand why he would write this, except that it meant that he still remembered me.

He wrote:

I was sick for a year at losing her. But now I have thought it over a lot and have learned much. . . . Beautiful as she was she felt instinctively that physically my need for her was not overpowering. In this respect she wanted me more than I wanted her. And as she was not a half way person, she hesitated and finally said, "No," we had better part.

This was not, of course, the reason for our parting. Again, his male chauvinism had come into play, so he would make of the parting one caused by my wanting him more than his wanting me. However, when he was eighty years old, he still remembered me and our love.

His biographer, Paul Buhle, writes:

He has recalled one precious incident from private life which speaks volumes. He knew his Trinidad relationship had definitely come to a close. And he spotted a woman, who regularly passed him on the street, dancing at a social event. Evidently beautiful, "she was much in demand." He asked to come and see her in her apartment. She readily agreed and when they shook hands "we never let go." On James' insistence he sought to have a discussion with her husband who declined to see him, James asked her to marry him and she "declined." Life had already become too precarious for intellectuals in the 1930's and the Black intellectual offered no solution. James retains the precious memory of her. "It is over forty years but I think we shall meet again. She will have put on a little weight and she will be a little gray but she will be as she was on that Monday morning, a human being made to order for another human being." 'But little sense of how a settled life might have developed out of such a liason, he had unconsciously chosen another way." Buhle, of course, is wrong in this because James did not choose the other way. It was I who walked away from him.

Buhle seems to suggest that I would have offered James only a bourgeois life, which would not have been true. Buhle adds "he had unconsciously chosen another way." Thus Buhle suggests further, that it was better we had not married, though he had no basis on which to judge this, and that it was James "consciously or unconsciously who had chosen another way." It was I who had found our love too costly physically.

I believe he kept the fond memory of me because he never had any responsibility toward me. I did not live with him. I did not have to ask him for money, for food, or for clothes or adjust to his schedule or to his moods. I worked companionably with him, then became his lover, so there was no disharmony. He probably felt that that was how the relationship of a man and a woman should be and perhaps used it as an example. On the other hand, as well as having two wives, he did have affairs, and these seemed to have been usually unhappy ones. Perhaps I did adjust to him. I certainly made no demands on him. If he had to go to meetings in other parts of the country, I accepted that with perfect equanimity. He did not like the fact that I returned to my husband, but he was prepared to accept it perhaps because it left him without any responsibilities. Yet he had said, very fiercely: "I should have had you as a virgin."

He wanted no other man to have had any part of me.

He often said, I understand, that he was sure that we would meet again. I wished too that that had happened. I am sure we would have been tremendously glad to have been with each other again, and it would have been a very happy meeting—a meeting based on many happy memories, and a meeting based on a recounting to each other what we had been doing and how we had both been faring since making love together in Harlem.

James describes himself in his cricket book as "a Puritan" and talks of his "Puritan soul," and of his learning the English Public School Code. He describes his family, including himself as "always present as the Puritan, the sense of discipline."

Did he really see himself a Puritan? If so, it would seem a charming innocence or, at the time it was written in the sixties, a desire to be known as "respectable." For his life was scarcely one of a Puritan. At one period, I understand, he was drinking heavily, when matters were not going well for him. There was also the subject of money. James was supported for most of his adult life by other people. Puritans would not condone such conduct. It would be regarded as a lack of self-respect, a lack of self-reliance. They would certainly disapprove of his many relationships.

Looking back over his politics and his writing, I am also reflecting on his relationships with other women. Probably the adjustments of marriage were too difficult for him; During his last years, when he was alone again, he seemed to be content to be an "eminence grise" among admirers.

I may sound somewhat critical now of C. L. R. I do not wish to be. He was a man of great ability, but I do not believe he was the superman that his last admirers made him to be.

My eldest grandson says I am an intellectual snob. I may well be and may well always have been. This means that I stand by my own standards of criticism; though I loved him, it does not mean that I should swoon over him. I am perhaps better able to judge than others who have been less close to him. It does not mean that I wish to lessen the proper acclaim he should receive. It does mean that I can look back and believe he could have attained a greater fame than he did because it would have been based on firmer grounds.

In regard to political positions, I always felt in discussing any event with Nello that my own view was as valid as his was. I met him as an equal. I think that was what made ours such a good relationship. For that is what it was: a man and a woman who met as equals. At least it was from my point of view. He would say later, "We met as two human beings coming together." For me it went further: A man and a woman who were in love and treated each other as equals.

I look back to the intervening years and to the different paths we each followed. We had a tie, a strong bond of remembrance; each of us held an end. When he was in his eighties, he still talked of me with affection to his biographer.

The suggestion that when we would meet again, a moment for which he was hoping, I would be a little grayer and a little heavier came from a letter from me to him. I remember my answering one of his letters and, in particular, remember I told him about my physical changes, so he would not expect me to look as I had as a young woman.

When he wrote to me another time, James said that when he went to the South for the first time, he noticed many white women eyeing him with definite interest as he passed. I remembered he had asked me in London, what did I feel when making eye contact with strangers in the street. These were invitations that could be followed up to make new "friends." For me with my upbringing, it was an extraordinary idea that I should look into the eyes of passersby.

Women were evidently often in his thoughts.

For instance, he talked of World War I, in which ten million men were killed. To illustrate one of its sad side effects, he talked of going to a party with a girl between twenty and thirty, in 1932. While he was sitting near her, she was accosted by a crude young man she did not know, who asked her to go out to dinner with him;

what he really intended was asking her to go to bed with him. The girl told James that such suggestions arose all the time. Why? Because there were too many women and too few men because of the toll of the war of 1914 to 1918.

Now if James had taken the Second World War and used Russia as an illustration, when twenty million men had been killed, then this number of women was important, he would have had a perfectly good example of one of the side effects of war. But both the young woman and James were wrong. This incident he said took place in 1932, that is, fourteen years after World War I ended. The boys who were ten then were now twenty-four, and those who were sixteen, now were thirty. We were heading toward a new war when a new crop of young men would be needed, so they were there ready in 1932. Simple arithmetic should have shown James this point against the war was incorrect. In any case there was so much that was terrible in war that it was an odd example to choose.

I may seem critical now of C. L. R. James in many ways. One reason is that I have never deviated from my support of Trotsky's analysis and view of history. This has meant a late recognition of a political division between us, though it never entered into our continuing friendship over the years because I was then not fully aware of his political positions.

Secondly, I feel he did not fulfill what could have given him a greater destiny; not the bolstered one he received with the adulation of his late admirers, but one as a key figure in the Caribbean.

For my own self and loves.

While I certainly do not have an admiring coterie around me in my old age, it does please me that the other men in my life always thought of me warmly.

My Zionist friend, Arthur, went to live in Tel Aviv, but when he returned to New York from time to time, he would pick me up in a fancy limousine and take me to lunch at a fancy restaurant. His son has been in touch with me in recent years, after his father's death. And he says: "You two would have been happy together."

He must have based this statement on his father's continuing feeling for me. For his father wrote to me ending his letters "always." Of course, a marriage between us would have been made impossible by our conflicting political view. In fancy, I think I would have enjoyed being the wife of an ambassador, hearing of high-level international intrigues.

My first husband wrote to me and sent me his books over the years. Usually, I answered briefly, so that a real correspondence between us would not develop: that would hurt my second husband.

I feel a woman has to have a loyalty to the man she marries as she would expect the man to have a loyalty to her; there must be an equal respect on both sides. But after the death of my second husband, my first one ended his last letter, before he died as follows: "Lots and lots of love. Take care of yourself."

My Russian thought that other men, except in the most ordinary social circumstances, should look on his wife only with respect. For him, infidelity was solely possible where true love existed, as in *Anna Karenina*.

I remained "faithful" to him for forty-three years until his death.

Before he died, my second husband was in a coma, but when I touched his cheek and said, "It's Louise," he gave a wide smile because I think he knew I was there.

So I retained to the end the love of all my men.

When James went back the last time to England and was established there again, he had a new coterie, but somehow by then, I believe he had been de-fanged, as it were. And although he was an excellent writer with a fine mind, a brilliant orator, and a participant in working-class disputes, my feeling is that he was no longer a danger to the country.

While he undoubtedly still went out and gave lectures on political matters from his own newly evolved political point of view to various audiences, he no longer was considered a revolutionary threat to the Establishment. This was a very different situation from when he was a young man. If he had been in England when the war broke out, he would have undoubtedly been imprisoned. In the States, he was deported and kept on Ellis Island. That fiery young man, however, had, it would seem, lost most of his fevor as he grew older.

When he was sent to Ellis Island for deportation, James appealed to Sir Anthony Eden to stop his deportation from the States. Amusedly, Sir Anthony replied that banishment to the United Kingdom could in no way be considered a punishment. Always C. L. R. had praise for the British. I could not understand his wanting to be an American. Was it the greater worship he received in the United States? Especially by women?

I wonder how his wives fared in that black-and-white situation in the United States. In many states it remained a crime for black and white persons to live together or to marry. There was one Declaration of Independence Day, with a group who had invited the mayor of Oakridge, Tennessee, to join, went on a lynching expedition of Negroes because one local black man was living in "sin" with a white woman.

I now fondly picture Nello sitting up in bed, books around him, watching soap operas as an old man. He said that when he was a child he would think it heaven if he could just lie in bed and read. I think then that he died happily. There were women in the house where he had his last room in Brixton, who would cook his food and bring it to him. Also, there were always admirers who came to see him and sit at his feet, as it were, as disciples. He needed too for a woman, not a wife, to be near, who would act as assistant, who would also bolster the assurance that he was and had been a great man throughout his life. He had this in Anne Grimshaw. She was, as we all were—that is, all of his women—intelligent. She was an anthropologist, a very fascinating field.

Buhle says that James dreaded, for at least his last twenty years, being left alone. He wanted admirers, especially women, around him. He did not want another marriage, but he did not want to be by himself.

It is different for me since now I am completely alone practically all my days, far from any member of my family, and I think that I am self-sufficient. I have books, that he too liked around him, and I continue to write. My days are occupied.

The publisher of *World Revolution*, writes of James in 1936:

> James himself was one of the most delightful and easy going personalities I have known, colorful, in more sense than one. A dark-skinned West Indian negro from Trinidad, he stood six-foot three in his socks and was noticeably good-looking. His memory was extraordinary. He could quote not only passages from Marxist classics but long extracts from Shakespeare in a soft lilting English, which was a delight to hear. Immensely amiable, he loved the flesh pots of capitalism: fine cooking, fine clothes, fine furniture *and beautiful women*. He had no trace of guilty remorse to be expected from a seasoned warrior of the class war.
>
> If politics was his religion, and Marx his God, if literature was his passion and Shakespeare his Prince amongst writers, cricket was his beloved activity. . . .
>
> Excess, perhaps was James' crime, and excess of words whose relevance to the contemporary tragedy was less than he supposed.

The first part of this description excellently describes the man I knew and was written at the time I knew him. I also agree with the second part. His admirers did not recognize that his words in speech and writing had less relevance to the tragedies of the world than he thought.

I do not think that James would have ever died for his cause or have gone to prison for his ideals as so many world leaders have.

Part Four
Commentary

13

James's Books

JAMES'S GREAT DESIRE WAS TO BECOME AN ACCEPTED WRITER; HE achieved that. By the end of his life, the critics were saying of his works:

> "James has been one of the most influential of West Indian writers."
> "*The Black Jacobins* 'is a classic and a book like none other.'"
> "C.L.R. James is one of the most remarkable writers of our generation." And of another book, "indispensable reading for whoever is interested in modern history and modern thinking."

James was also a scholarly man: he could read Greek and Latin and French. He knew the English classics and the French classics from the time he was a young man, and he never ceased to reread them. His interests in the success of books was illustrated when he once asked me, many years later, how my first husband was faring as a writer. My husband, like myself had started life anxious to be a literary writer. However, he could not make a living by it and had to write popular books; one of them sold three million copies. It was of course, not in any way, a literary effort. However, James seemed very impressed, and also because the book had been made into a movie and later on was used on television. I myself was not impressed at all, so that I was a little astonished that James could be.

James, by the end of his life, had the critics attribute to him really serious praise.

One wrote:

> "C.L.R. James is a 20th century giant in thought and deed."
> "James is amongst the great of the 20th century."

He wrote only two full-length political books: *The Black Jacobins* and *World Revolution: 1917–1936*. There are three further volumes of his speeches, essays, pamphlets, which have been gathered together.

His other early books included *The Life of Captain Cipriani*. This is the story of a white Corsican man who organised trade unions in Trinidad. The last three chapters of the book were taken from it and issued as *A History of Negro Revolt*. He also brought with him, from Trinidad, the manuscript of *Minty Alley*, which was published in London.

During his period with the Johnson/Forest group, he collaborated with others in some pamphlets. The most important was *State Capitalism and World Revolution* with Grace Lee and Raya Dunayevskaya. He also wrote a pamphlet: *Notes on Dialectics*. After his meeting with others to see Trotsky, he had written with the Socialist Workers' Party's support, an article for their journal, which was later printed as a booklet: *The Negro Question in the United States*. Most of these articles and pamphlets were political, as the titles show. They added up to a considerable amount of writing, but they were not books in the accepted sense.

In his thirties and in the Thirties, James wrote: *Captain Cipriani;* his only novel, *Minty Alley;* his finest book, *The Black Jacobins;* his play, *Toussaint L'Ouverture;* his long book on major events of the time, *World Revolution: 1917 to 1936*. This was the period in which I was closely associated with him. This was his period of greatest output of books. He also discussed with me his idea of writing a book based on *Moby Dick*. At the same time, we were discussing and writing articles for *FIGHT*, and for the *New Leader* and the I.L.P. interparty, paper *Controversy*. So this was the James I knew and knew intimately his writings. He liked me to review all that he wrote.

In the Forties and his Forties, James produced in collaboration with others, some political pamphlets. I did not see them nor know about them except for the unexplained arrival of the thin journal *Spartacus*, by which I learned James, under the name of Johnson, had turned anti-Trotsky.

In the Fifties, and his Fifties, James produced a new book, *Mariners, Renegades and Castaways*, his long contemplated work on Melville's saga of the search for the white whale.

In the Sixties, James wrote *Beyond a Boundary*. These were two books in two decades. He wrote a large number of articles and some other pamphlets. He sent me the major ones including three speeches given in Trinidad, printed as *Modern Politics*.

I started writing again in the Sixties when he left off.

We had both produced anti-colonial work. He in a section of *Captain Cipriani* which was published as a pamphlet, *The Need for Self-*

Government, and I a whole book on *Puerto Rico: The Case For Independence.*

James started writing early. I too started writing before my "teens': such sad, sad stories that would make everyone want to be good and the world a better place. I was a very priggish girl.

My first published writing was when I was about sixteen or seventeen. *The Daily Express* held a nation-wide competition on the best essay on *"What Is Happiness?"*

I won second prize. The newspaper sent a reporter to interview the winner. They did not send anyone to interview me. I think if they had done so, they would have been surprised I was so young. I had just been expelled from school before what would normally be the finishing age.

I still remember how I started off my essay though I do not remember the rest of it. And I did not then, nor have ever since, been one to keep clippings about my writings or activities.

I began quoting Omar Khayyam:

> "To him who desireth much
> much is given:
> "To him who desireth little
> little is given:
> *But neither according to the letter of his desire,"*

I wonder for both James and myself how much of this became true.

I believe the prize was twenty-five pounds. The winner received a hundred.

At the university my professors thought I would do well as a writer. It was a "dizzy" time for me.

All through the years, in the States, when I was financially unable to do so, I wanted very much to get back to being a writer.

When my husband and I retired to Puerto Rico, I found there was a Socialist Party, a Communist Party, one or two more radical groups, a nationalist Party, and to my surprise, a very small Trotskyist Party. The head of it was Juan Antonio Corretger, a gentle elderly man; a poet. I would very much have liked to have met him, and to end my life with a Trotskyist political group. Unfortunately by then, I already had an incurable heart disease. It did not kill me, but it meant that I had to be completely inactive. However, I did my part in the only way I was then able to do so, by writing books advocating the independence of Puerto Rico. I was still a Trotskyist in thought as I had been when I knew Nello.

So after the long period when I was freed from the financial ties of my son's large family, I had gone back to political activity. When I say political activity I mean that I was once again working for "La Causa" in my writings. My political books were sold through the universities, the university libraries, so that I hoped that what I wrote did and will continue to have an effect. The books had as their objective the call for the independence of Puerto Rico. In all, I had ten books published: only two of them about Puerto Rico were a-political. The rest dealt with the various problems of the island as a colony of the United States. They were issued by well-known North American publishers and distributed mainly through the States and Puerto Rico.

I helped C.L.R. during our early time together with his writings, not doing any of my own except for articles for our paper and later for the I.L.P. paper.

As I have said, I helped him with the editing and proof reading of *Minty Alley* for which he expressed appreciation in a signed copy.

I aided too in *World Revolution,* though there his main assistant was Harry Wicks.

But I helped mostly with *The Black Jacobins.* For me that is his best work not because I was with him at the time or gave some aid but because I felt it was the best expression of himself. I wish he had gone on to write a dozen such books of those troubled, enchanted islands of the Caribbean.

But he went a different path and I too followed a different path. When I remember his writings, it is with *The Black Jacobins* that I associate him.

When I was working for him on *The Black Jacobins,* I never managed to get one of the comfortable blue leather desks in the Reading Room, under the huge dome of the British Museum, but always sat at one of the small ones wedged in between them.

James himself, of course, went to the museum for his research too, but somehow we never made the expedition together.

I often wondered how he could write such a fine book on Haiti without going to that island to see it. But, of course, he knew his own Caribbean island, where the conditions for the black slaves had, in the past, been the same. It was the people he knew rather then the terrain.

It was his own heritage. He knew the position of the black slaves on the sugar plantation, for they had been the same on his own island. In their rage, he was at one with them, for this was the rage of his own ancestors. The role too of the Creoles was the same in Trinidad as it had been in Haiti.

For me, *The Black Jacobins* is his finest book. He is conveying his own feelings about his own people and their history. He is looking back to his own roots.

In *The Atlantic Slave Trade and Slavery,* written years later in 1970, in *Amistad,* he writes;

"Besides the oppression of the master himself, his laws and his overseers, the slaves were oppressed by their limited knowledge of the world outside the plantation. Masters felt that a slave who learned how to read and write would lose his proficiency of picking worms off tobacco leaves or of chopping cotton, so thoroughly had slavery separated thought and feeling from work. . . . But the capacities of men were always leaping out of the confinements of the system. Always with one eye cocked on the door, the slaves learned how to read and write."

He sent it to me knowing I would see it in relation to his famous book, and when I had been at his side and helping as I could by going to the British Museum to do some research, and in daily watching his masterpiece build, sentence by sentence, theme by theme, action by action, I am sorry also, I did not keep the accompanying letter he sent me. I am sorry that along the years, I lost the copy he had inscribed to me with his gratitude.

My copy of *Minty Alley* I gave to Professor Robert Hill, his literary executor. He had also written on the fly-leaf his gratitude to me for my help.

When I was proofreading *Minty Alley,* I felt it was very much a first novel, and was somewhat surprised that Nello had been able to get it published. My literary standards were high. After all, my aim had previously been to be a literary writer. Nello had made some contacts with the Bloomsbury set when he was first in London. It was through the help of Leonard and Virginia Wolfe and their self-owned Hogarth Press that it was published.

My only contact with the Bloomsbury Set was when I had been sent by a woman's group to write about the unusual nursery of Sacheverell Sitwell's baby. What was most unusual was that the baby had a black nanny. In England, this was unknown.

Years Later, *Minty Alley* was portrayed by his followers as a book about working class people. There is one scene very vivid still in my mind; a middle-aged, not fully qualified nurse, stands in her doorway and makes a small boy crawl on his belly over the street to her. She holds a switch in her hand. The child is terrified each inch of the way as he moves toward her, knowing she is going to start whipping him unmercifully as soon as he reaches her. The book's hero stands fascinated and sick watching her. He knows he should interfere but is too weak to do so.

She and other characters were not working class people to my mind, but lumpen proleterian, the source from which Fascists make their recruits. In regard to James' other early book, Captain Cipriani, this had been a white man not a Black man organizing a workers' movement against the government. I knew C.L.R. when he was still a young man. However, his two most important books were written when I was with him. I do not mean in any way to suggest that my being with him had in any way helped in this achievement, although I did help in research for the *Black Jacobins*.

James's book *World Revolution: 1917 to 1936,* was published in 1937. In it James wrote that Trotsky personified the principles of Marxism and Leninism. He had obviously hoped Trotsky would give the book his acclaim and the fact that he did not may have been a factor in James' break with Trotsky.

As well, there were numerous prophecies that James made in the book which turned out to be erroneous.

This is not to say that the book was not, at the time, an excellent analysis of the European situation. Buhle writes of the brilliant analysis and power of James' book written in 1937. *The London Times,* however, in a review was scathing about the book, called it "jejune" and suggested "Mr. James could make the effort to conceive it possible that he might be mistaken."

In regard to the war, James rightly believed that Hitler could not win. He also could write wrongly, "Capitalism, after climbing great heights, came to a standstill and has slipped from its foundations . . . through it all, the general line is clear, the objective hopelessness of the profit system."

James' books and his politics were naturally intertwined. When he wrote *World Revolution 1917–1936,* he was a Trotskyist, praising Trotsky: believing in Lenin's theory of the necessity of a party of vanguard cadres; and believing in Marxism and the necessity for class struggle.

When he wrote his pamphlets with the Johnson/Forest group, he was attempting to evolve political theories of his own, not based on those of the three whose advocate he had been, even though they were meant to be new studies in Marxism.

I remained and still remain loyal to the ideas of Trotsky, a great man with whom I could have been close, but had mistakenly missed the opportunity. There has been no deviation for me from the theories James and I had once upheld together.

But James journeyed down several different political paths.

When I heard of Trotsky's assassination, I was wrought with grief.

JAMES'S BOOKS 165

Though I was not active in the movement, I was still ideologically attached to it. From where would we now get guidance?

I thought of James at that moment, not as a leader, but as someone with whom I could share my grief. I had no one. I would have liked then to have been in touch with him or with one of our old group. Letters from him came later.

Despite having moved away from Trotsky, James did write a tribute to Trotsky on his death.

Lenin had written of the joining of workers and peasants: this was a precarious union and that it "will break down." In fact both he and Trotsky were looking in the future to a revolution in Germany, a highly industrialized nation, with Germany then taking the industrial lead, and Russia providing the "Bread Basket" for the world. Marx says the proletariat and the peasants are two distinct classes often in opposition.

In *World Revolution: 1917–1936*, which James wrote while with our group, he made many mistakes in his analysis. He was sure that a French Revolution at the time would be successful. He expected revolutions all over the world after World War II, including Britain. He also took stands on politics then that he later totally discarded.

He wrote: "The first law of Stalinism is to praise Stalin. The second is to abuse Trotsky."

He succumbed to the second law.

He made it part of Stalin's deliberate plan, in this early book, for Hitler to come to power. Trotsky and most other political analysts have always believed this to be quite wrong.

He also could say in 1936:

"The Stalinists are approaching the end of their boom period."

Yet all over the world for a considerable period of time the Communist Parties continued to have considerable influence. They still do in France and Italy, and some other European countries.

The political break with Trotskyism meant in reality a break with both Leninism and Marxism, though James, on and off still declared himself a Marxist.

Two other books to build up his output were *The Future In The Present,* Selected writings: volume One. *Spheres of Existence,* Selected writings: Volume Two. *At The Rendevous of History,* Selected writings: Volume Three.

On the whole, James produced a limited amount of work about blacks:

James wrote *The Black Jacobins* about Haiti, an authoritive book, in 1936, then a play based on it. He wrote articles on the Abyssinian War; on the Slave Trade; on Trinidadian *George Padmore: Black*

Marxist Revolutionary; on International African Affairs; on the Ghana Revolution; two lenghty pamphlets, *Modern Politics and Party Politics in the West Indies,* on Trinidad; *A National Purpose for Caribbean People.*

One article evolved from his meeting with others from the Socialist Workers' Party with Trotsky: *The Revolutionary Answer to the Negro Problem in the United States:* The text of a talk by him was called *Black Studies and the Contemporary Student.* This was mimeographed when he was teaching at Federal City University in Washington, D.C. I am not in any way trying to lessen his interest in the black movement in general, in Africa and in the Caribbean, though this was not basic work for him, but surprised that he wrote so little about the special black situation in the United States where he lived for over twenty-five years, and must have seen and experienced the terrible degradation and discrimination of blacks. He was in the United States in the late Sixties when the black Civil Rights movement was in full swing. He took no part in it. He excused himself to his students saying he could not talk because he was on a visitor's visa. So U.S. blacks, in general, do not know his name.

At first, his main interest was in Marxism. He worked with white colleagues and he loved and married white women. His adherents were, black and white intellectuals but neither black nor white workers.

Looking back, I realize, that while he did have influence with some Africans and West Indians, he lacked support amongst black and white working-class masses, except possibly in Trinidad, and then not much to be permanently influential there.

Perhaps he had had influence more in Antigua than elsewhere, not so much directly as through an admirer he had met in Canada, where he lived for a short time on leaving Trinidad after his defeat in elections there. But influence in the U.S. was another matter.

He could say in a speech in 1981:

"In regard to Black people in the United States . . . mentally and spiritually they have left the ghetto. They may be compelled to live there because you cannot leave the ghetto unless you have somewhere else to go. But they have left it. I do not believe any forces exist in the United States today to drive them back. They are out of it and going to remain out of it."

I find this a very extraordinary statement.

When he edited *The Nation,* organ of Eric Williams's People's National Movement in Trinidad, the paper included articles of a general nature, such as literary reprints, pieces about cricket, carnival and calypso. There was even one special supplement celebrating Abraham Lincoln. As editor, he would not criticize the North American held Chaguamas Base.

According to Paul Buhle:

"He would not assail American imperialism nor threaten to overturn capitalism," though these were stands made by all other West Indian "left wingers."

A comparison might be made between the work of James and that of Frantz Fanon, another West Indian writer from Martinique. He was born in 1925. At the age of twenty-seven, he had published *Black Skin, White Mask*. Then came L'An V. de Revolution Algerisienne (in English, *A Dying Colonialism*). Last was *The Wretched of the Earth*, finished just before he died, in 1961, a young man of thirty-six.

The last one has a lengthy preface by Jean Paul Sartre.

James wrote his two full length anticolonialism and antiimperialism books during the time we were working together.

C.L.R. James did not write in his long life, three such full length anti-colonial, black movement books, as Frantz Fanon had done in his short life.

In regard to the crimes of colonialism, it is said James indeed went straight to the core of imperial ideology, and took it on effectively, as an absence of fair-play.

Fair play is not in the lexicon of revolutionaries.

James speaks to an audience about *State Capitalism and World Revolution*, published collectively by his Johnson/Forest group in 1950, and also published in book form while he was living once more in England, in 1956.

He says:

" . . . that stands substantially today as the best analysis you can find anywhere . . . political analysis of the development of the Russian revolution."

That is his own evaluation. But as in his first book on *World Revolution*, his analysis in this second book, on *World Revolution* was wrong, by any Marxist standards, that state capitalism existed in the U.S.S.R. Capitalism is producing a product for a profit by an industrialist or a corporation. State capitalism is products being made for a profit by the state. In the Soviet Union products were, in the main, produced not for profit but for the needs of the people: food, housing, medical care and supplies, education, were all produced at a loss for the benefit of the people. The fact that Stalin used harshly cruel methods, to enforce them, was a dictator without humanism; allowed a bureaucracy to grow whose only function was to support him in power, and deny human rights and any dissidence to authority, did not alter the economic foundations of the revolution. Power was a motive but not profit. Few factories or industries made much of a profit, nor did the collective farms. By ensuring total employment all such enterprises were over-staffed and financially inefficient and unprofitable.

There were then C.L.R.'s two a-political books: *Mariners, Renegades and Castaways,* James' book about Herman Melville's *Moby Dick*, and his much acclaimed cricket book, *Beyond A Boundary*.

The first was written while he was still in the United States: the second when he returned to England and was once more acting as a cricket reporter for *The Manchester Guardian;* continuing his lifetime interest in the game.

When he was deported, in 1952, to Ellis Island, he wrote while alone, the apolitical book he had had in mind for some years that was his book on Herman Melville's *Moby Dick*.

He had discussed this book with me in London. I could not quite understand his absorption with it. I did not see it as an allegory of the world and its tensions, and I am doubtful if he had such thoughts about it then, because we were so close at that time, he would have expounded his theories to me.

When we discussed the idea, it was as man's struggle against Fate, and how his own obsessions could destroy him. It did turn out somewhat differently when he got down to writing *Mariners, Renegades and Castaways* in the solitude of his incarceration.

James' book on Melville's *Moby Dick,* is supposed to have become an allegory for the whole modern world and its tensions. I do not believe many people who read the book see it in these terms. "No one but Melville," James emphasizes, "anticipated that the executives of the ruling class would themselves go mad."

During his incarceration, his thoughts turned from politics, when I would have thought his ordeal would have made him agressively anti-North American: make him think of himself as *Inside the Monster* as José Martí, the Cuban patriot, wrote.

Instead, there is a rather unpleasant incident.

He had been greatly helped during his internment by an old Jewish communist. Instead of feeling grateful, James harshly dissociated himself from his benefactor when talking to the authorities, probably hoping to gain their favour and to their relenting and letting him stay in the United States. Even his admirer Paul Buhle suggests this was not a worthy action.

In *Claridad,* the weekly periodical of the Puerto Rican Socialist Party, in October, 1991, a Mexican author wrote on the *Resurrection of Herman Melville.* The article covered his life briefly and showed how his *Moby Dick* had come to be recognized as a masterpiece, a hundred years after his death. Names of various authors who had dealt with his work were given. I looked to see if C.L.R. James' was amongst them. It was not mentioned.

In regard to his *Notes on Dialectics,* I subscribed for a long time to *Contempory Marxism,* later to be labelled *Social Justice.* These were thick quarterly journals, seriously written mostly by professors from prestigious U.S. universities. Over several years, there was never a quotation from, nor a reference made, to C.L.R. James' book or to him as a Marxist.

Of course, by that time he was not, once he had given up being a Trotskyist; but from time to time he continued to say that he was.

In five gathered reviews of James's work listed in *C.L.R. James: At The Rendevous of Victory,* only one is a book about Africa. This is *Nkrumah and the Ghana Revolution.* Part One of this was written in 1958. Part Two includes a speech delivered in Accra in 1960. Part Three is a letter to Nkrumah written in 1962, and Part Four, two articles published in the *Trinidad Evening News.* Other material is from Ghanian political journal and a further extract from an article on *Pan African Revolt.* This string of articles and extracts with an Introduction totaled two hundred twenty-four pages. It is in this review that C.L.R. James is called "one of the most remarkable writers of our generation," and in another review, "A crucial piece of work. No student of African history should be without it."

But again, it was not a book as such but a compilation of articles, pamphlets and speeches.

Notes on Dialectics, written in 1949, was circulated within the Johnson/Forest group. It was issued twenty years later by Robert Hill, Canada, 1965: fifteen years later in a book which included *Modern Politics* and *Facing Reality.*

James is said, in his own eyes at the end of his life, to have been a faithful disciple of Marxism and of Lenin. Since during his late years, he wanted to abolish the political party, he was certainly a Leninist no longer. He also wrote that "Marxism was discredited in the world," so he was no longer a Marxist.

James impressed upon his listeners, "the lessons of personal development, understanding of culture and faith in an undying potentiality of mass movements across the world."

To believe in the undying potentiality of mass movements across the world is very fine and idealistic, but it does not define what these mass movements should be. The potentiality of a mass movement could as easily be one of Fascism as of any social revolution. The followers of Hitler were the majority of Germans.

In his review of the Hungarian Revolution in *Facing Reality,* by James in 1958, Paul Buhle for the first time seems critical, for he says the text approached as close as ever to an anarchist philosophy. In fact, a great deal of this later philosophy was anarchistic. James' insistence that it was the masses that needed to make a revolution is undoubtedly true and one that has never been denied. In fact Trotsky says, "It is the masses that makes the engine go." That is without the masses there could be no revolution. But no leadership, no government is the doctrine of Nihilists such as advocated by Kropotkin.

With his book on *American Civilization,* fairly recently published, his third wife Selma Weinstein helped him with it. It was conceived between the two of them, and she was aiding him in getting material for the book in 1958 and 1959. The book was published in 1992. This was after his death when praise of him began to rise.

In the Introduction, James is presented as a man of tremendous influence in the world and a man of tremendous wisdom.

Leaving that aside, these thoughts of James when he was fifty, at middle-age and having spent fifteen years in the United States, are of interest. He meant these notes to be a rough draft for a lengthy book. He "makes a considerable use of quotations throughout the book." He suggests that they should be eliminated because they were taking up too much of the manuscript. He obviously wrote this as a draft to show to a publisher. He did show it when he was in England, after having been deported from the States, to his early publisher of *World Revolution,* that is Secker and Warburg, but Warburg turned it down. Warburg has said of his earlier writing that James had an excess of words and many of them were not as relevant as he thought.

But he was to find another publisher later.

James's views are however, of interest, and not only because they are the thoughts of and the summing up of North American civilisation by a man who had lived there twenty years, but of particular interest of a West Indian who had lived there for twenty years. To me they were of particular interest because this was a period when, while he had continued to have some thoughts of me and we had had some contact, it was a time I know very little about the paths that he was following.

A quotation is given in the Introduction which was a statement that James made in an interview with Anna Grimshaw in 1986.

James says

"Cricket had plunged me into politics long before I was aware of it. When I did turn to politics, I did not have much to learn."

I myself do not see the relevance of that statement and know that he had a great deal to learn, because we learned about politics over a period of five years together. Concerning too the situation in North America, the period immediately following the American Revolution, that is in 1776, James writes:

"America, at the time, presents a spectacle of economic and social equality unknown in history. No one is very rich, no one is very poor. Opportunity is open to all. Thus in actually living conditions, America is unique."

The social conditions embodied the ideal conditions for bourgeois individualism. All individuals start level; prizes go to the energetic and the thrifty. All fit into "The Mold." It is not necessary for me to query this statement. Anyone who has read North American history knows that this suggestion, that there was no division between rich and poor at that period is not true.

I see then this man whom I had known and worked with over five years from the beginning of his political development, and along a path that we had travelled together, arriving after his first stay in the United States, coming to the conclusion that when they broke from England, the new colonies represented almost a classless society. In the next one or two sentences he changes this a little, but he has made the categorical statement of his vision of the birth of this new nation of which he was anxious to become a citizen. He says that the United States allows the ideals of the 18th century of Europe to be expressed in a manner closely approximating them.

James says that between 1783 and 1835, America shows the ideal conditions for which Europe struggled so hard. Nevertheless, James quotes De Tocqueville:

"There is a total lack of any free discussion in the United States. In no country," he says emphatically, "is there such a lack of free and independent discussion."

In this comparison between the old Europe and the new country of North America, my own quotation from De Tocqueville would further be:

"Absolute monarchists have dishonored despotism; let us beware lest democratic republics should re-instate it."

But James does go into the history of the past which is rightly very necessary for an understanding of the present.

I will quote too from two other black men of importance living in the same period as James.

Malcolm X said:

"When you deal with the past you are dealing with history, you are dealing actually with the origin of the thing. When you know the origin, you know the cause. If you don't know the cause, it is impossible for you and me to have a clear mind in this society without going into the past."

Then Sir Philip Sherlock, who was Secretary General of the Association of Caribbean Universities said, "If you don't know the past, you don't have much future."

In this way James does do what is necessary in a survey of *American Civilization,* that is he goes into the past history in the States and the roots from which most Americans have come into from Europe.

While this is necessary and desirable and I applaud it, I would suggest that James does not analyze history from any Marxist position. It is not obligatory, but James had been a Marxist.

Of the American literary writers, James deals almost wholly with Walt Whitman and Herman Melville. He quotes great passages from the former: in fact several pages of the book are given up just to reproduce some of Whitman's poems. The material on Herman Melville undoubtedly led to James's book on *Moby Dick.* He had already done some research on this, and so was able when he was on Ellis Island, to continue and make this into one of his books.

Oddly, he pays little attention to Mark Twain, who is always considered the writer "par excellence" of homegrown American literature, reflecting the American character, the American world and ideals.

How far James had wandered from the intellectual path pursued in the days when he and I were still young is shown in his summing up of the culture of Americans: He sees it in their popular music, in their comics, their cinema, their television. It is his own personal theory.

His cricket book, *Beyond the Boundary,* he sent to my brother. He also sent me *Amistad I,* in which he had an excellent article on the *African Slave Trade*. This was published in 1970, a year later, but I do not know when I received it.

I did not send him any of my books except *The Spanish Caribbean* at his request. This might have been because my husband would have been upset had I done so. Also, I somehow never sent my books around to friends. I never thought of it. Now they are out of print and I have only one or two copies of each.

In his book on cricket, which brought James into the limelight in England and then in the States, he deals with cricketers, with poets, philosophers and artists, more than he does with politics or with revolutionaries. He suggests that the fielding of a ball, the hitting of a ball, a stroke, will take us to a far more fundamental consideration of life, and that the response to physical action or vivid representation of it, is necessary, because we are made that way. For unknown centuries survival for us, like all other animals depended upon competent and effective physical activity. He says further, another name for the perfect flow of motion is style, or if you will, significant form. In another place he writes, "professionalism, will produce the poetic, artistic, or philosophical qualities which will make the great athlete and the great cricketer of the future." He makes the suggestion that the case of West Indian self-government—and "it is not cricket"—"have come together:" That is, that the need for self-government and the fair-play as shown in cricket on the English playing fields.

He writes of the British people "that they were never very forthcoming, still the British people represented the ideal of what I was doing. That was the British I knew." So in this book on cricket, he links cricket to the English sense of fair-play. A shopkeeper in England had advanced him one hundred pounds to go to Paris to do research on his book on Toussaint L'Ouverture, and again he speaks of him as having the "sterling British Character." He never mentions the British class system.

Though cricket is a widespread popular sport in England, it is really an upper and middle-class sport. The working-class game is "soccer"—football. I do not think James ever mentioned it, though he played it occasionally when young. Probably he would not have encountered it as a serious sport until he went to Lancashire, England. Certainly he did not follow the results of the games, when in London. In the States, he was undoubtedly only peripherally interested in North American basketball, football, or baseball. He said he had read one book on baseball "and never read another." yet these games provide blacks with many opportunities to become national heroes. Sports are one of the few areas open to them for upward mobility. He did, during his last illness in bed, ask to be brought a book about Willie Mays. Perhaps this was the one book mentioned earlier.

His cricket book is partly autobiographical. He tells us a great deal about himself and his later changed political views. In *BEYOND A. BOUNDARY,* James idealizes early Greece. In James's enthusiasm for the Greek city states, which produced such as amazing collection of sculptors, philosophers, playwrights, and mathematicians, he neglects the fact that they were built on slavery. Neither slaves nor women had the franchise in Athens.

In industrial countries of the West, people of some wealth can live a good life. They have the money to buy paintings, books, seats to the Opera and the concert halls, and study at the top universities. They too know or can know about the facts of 'real politiks.' It is the mass of the people without wealth, who lack these advantages and who have votes that are only phantom tokens of democracy. They are the industrial slaves of the system.

Among James's admirers are many intelligent intellectual, well educated people, but I would dearly like to see a Marxist analysis of his work.

I found recently that we both had had almost identical titles to works we had written.

He wrote a pamphlet called *From Toussaint to Castro* (1962). Mine was the subtitle of my book on *The Spanish Caribbean— From Columbus to Castro* (1979).

Actually James makes only one short mention of Castro in the article: "I do not propose to plunge into the turbulent waters of controversy about Cuba. I have written about the West Indies in general and Cuba is the most West Indian island in the West Indies. That suffices."

I give whole chapters to Castro since I cover the growth and development of the three Spanish islands over five hundred years to the present day.

James visited Cuba once with a group and during a meeting with them with Castro, he was taken aside and given a private interview. As far as I know, James never wrote about it, and never wrote about the great accomplishments Castro has made in the island.

According to United Nations statistics, Cuba has the highest medical standards for its people than in the whole Western Hemisphere including the United States. It also has the highest standard of literacy in the Western Hemisphere including the United States. From a country when Castro took over of about 80 percent illiteracy, it now has over 80% literacy.

I have made two short visits to Cuba since Castro took over and am enormously impressed by his accomplishments. I never had had the opportunity to meet or see Castro. I did talk to the Vice-Secretary for Cultural Affairs, a charming, highly cultured man.

James and I also wrote on a similar subject about North American naval bases in the Caribbean.

He wrote a lengthy article supporting the Prime Minister's decision to renew the lease on Chaguaramas Base. Williams was doing this for practical reasons at the time. Nello wrote the piece for him though he himself objected to the policy.

I wrote a whole book, *Calamity in the Caribbean: Nuclear Bombs in Puerto Rico,* urging the removal of the United States Navy out of Roosevelt Roads since it was an ever present danger to all the people of the island and was there without their consent, without payment and by right of conquest only.

14
James's Political Paths

JAMES'S BOOKS AND HIS POLITICS WERE NATURALLY INTERTWINED when he wrote *World Revolution*. He was a Trotskyist, praising Trotsky, believing in Lenin's theory of the necessity of a party of vanguard cadres, and believing in Marxism and the necessity for class struggle.

When he wrote his pamphlets with the Johnson/Forest group, he was attempting to evolve political theories of his own, not based on those of the three whose advocate he had been, even though they were meant to be new studies in Marxism.

I remained and still remain loyal to the ideas of Trotsky, a great man with whom I could have been close, but had mistakenly missed the opportunity. There has been no deviation for me from the theories James and I had once upheld together.

But James journeyed down several different political paths.

When I heard of Trotsky's assassination, I was wrought with grief. Though I was not active in the movement, I was still ideologically attached to it. From where would we now get guidance?

I thought of James at that moment, not as a leader, but as someone with whom I could share my grief. I had no one. I would have liked then to have been in touch with him or with one of our old group.

Despite having moved away from Trotsky, James did write a tribute to Trotsky on his death.

From being a Trotskyist, he moved to a Trotskyist "Tendency," which was a belief that state capitalism existed in the U.S.S.R. There was then a brief rejoining of the Trotskyist group. After this, he made several turns, he decided on a political policy in which there was to be no political party. By this concept he cut himself off from Leninism. He wanted only spontaneous uprisings and "councils" instead of a party. He denounced Marxism as dead. He went off into other personal political paths, making at least three separate turns. His politics, then, had become volatile.

As I see it, he had no solid guidelines any more to offer his followers, though he would at times, claim he was still a Marxist.

It must not be forgotten that these were war years of the Johnson/Forest group, and here was James, except for a few anti-war speeches given to blacks, hiding away as an intellectual recluse. His anti-war efforts in the States were certainly small. It was an odd time to be going into a study of Marxism and dialecticalism.

When James, for the second time, broke with the Socialist Workers' Party in 1950, he and his followers thought that Trotskyism was dead. However, it still has today small parties in Europe and in Africa, and in the Caribbean, M.P's in England.

Even Buhle admits that James took his little group, at that time, "into the wilderness."

When he was in the States, there was Schachtman, Eastman, Cannon, Spectre, who were the leaders of the Trotskyist movement, who were the editors of the Trotskyist papers, and who made the policy. I think this too may well have been one of the reasons for James's break with the group, that he had to be a leader. He would, rather than make a contribution in a larger sphere, have preferred to have only three or four people around him, and that grew to his own reckoning, only to a dozen people, and another little coterie, but of which he was definitely the leader and which was comprised mainly of admiring women.

Raya Dunayevskaya's idea was the Soviet Society as a form of state capitalism. Capitalism means the offering of services of goods for profit. In the Soviet Union there were numerous services that were free: education and medical programs: rents were low, a fraction of costs, so was transportation, and basic foods. Many industries were operating at losses. How could then the word capitalism be applied?

This then was his first move away from Trotskyism: a belief that the U.S.S.R. was no longer a socialist state. From then on James's political views took a zigzag course from a Trotskyist to a position that was close to being anarcho-syndicalist.

About the invitation that James had of visiting the United States, it is suggested that our small group sought to remove an oddball "troublemaker," who was their deepest thinker and most popular figure. Buhle is talking about the group to which I belonged, and I can assure him and his co-admirers that we never thought of James as a trouble-maker. We always acknowledged his leadership in the group and were grateful for his oratory skills. But on the other hand we were far from being the idolizers of James that he became in his Johnson/Forest group. We acknowledged him as a leader of the group, we certainly had no desire for him to leave us, but we nevertheless felt and talked to him as an intellectual equal. I think that this was so by almost every member of the group; not all, but most of the young students were down from Oxford and Cambridge, and from London University. We listened to his views, he listened to ours, and we were all supporters of Trotsky. Trotsky was the one whose suggestions politically we followed. We certainly would never have put James on a level with Trotsky. When he was writing *World Revolution*, we all did our best to help him by looking up sources, by finding clippings that would be useful. In fact, we did a great deal of the donkey work of research, and he was also helped considerably, something which his later admirers have never mentioned, by the assistance of Harry Wicks, who had been a very early Communist and who changed over to Trotskyism.

In his book *World Revolution: 1917–1936,* James supported the necessity of a revolutionary party.

He wrote:

"The successful leadership of a revolutionary party, collective or individual, is the work of creative genius."

This meant he believed in the genius of Lenin and Trotsky.

He also wrote in that book, that in the 1918 revolutionary situation in Germany, the leadership of Rosa Luxemburg and Karl Liebnecht "lacked the organised party's training and experience," which would have given them a probable victory instead of failure.

Contrary to these earlier views, he later expounded new ideas extolling leaderless, spontaneous uprisings.

"The party formula has been exhausted. It cannot work any longer," he wrote.

When he attested to the need of a vanguard party, he was a Trotskyist. When he denied it, he denied Leninism too, for one of Lenin's principal axioms was the need of a strictly controlled party. It was the point on which the Russian revolutionaries split into Bolsheviks and Mensheviks in 1905.

James wanted always to evolve his own ideas. He was to call for the uprising of the masses without the benefit of the party and the intellectuals. He wrote as if earlier leaders had ignored the masses.

Trotsky wrote in his *History of the Russian Revolution:*

"At those crucial moments when the old order becomes no longer endurable to the masses, they break over the barriers excluding them from the political area, sweep aside their traditional representatives, and create by their own interference, the initial groundwork for a new regime ... The history of a revolution is for us, first of all, a history of the forcible entrance of the masses into the realm of rulership over their own destiny."

Unfortunately in all the post-war situations, the masses were thrown back by the military of the ruling classes.

For James to suggest that the masses had to make the revolution was so obvious, no one had ever thought otherwise. James, however, would call for the uprising of the masses of workers without the benefit of the party and the intellectual leadership.

Trotsky wrote that the end of Stalin's policy in the U.S.S.R. would be the restoration of capitalism in Russia. James states strongly that Trotsky was wrong. He wrote: "Trotsky's conception that they (the U.S.S.R. people) were going to join the bourgeoisie once more was entirely wrong."

Alas, today we know that Trotsky's prophecy was right.

In the 1905 revolution the workers and peasants organized the Soviets. This was similar, I imagine, to what James wanted as the councils of people. The Soviets were renewed in the 1917 revolution, but if it had not been for Lenin and Trotsky, the revolution would have stopped in February, and Kerensky would have taken over and Kerensky would have brought back the White Army for repression of the people.

While James spent a number of years writing notes on dialectics, it must be remembered that Trotsky, who had spent a lifetime studying Marx and Engels, and who had had a practical experience of the revolution, felt that James' understanding of dialecticism was faulty.

James's first political book was *World Revolution 1917–1936*. He asked Trotsky to write an introduction and Trotsky did not answer, and in fact made his remark privately to one of the young Trotskyist about its lack of real understanding of *Dialecticism*. I wonder if this was not the reason why James himself felt that he had to write such a book *Notes on Dialectics,* so as to prove Trotsky wrong.

For many years I subscribed to a journal written by Marxist intellectuals entitled *Modern Marxism,* and later *Social Justice*. All the articles were excellently written and resourced. I never saw in all this years any reference to C. L. R. James as a Marxist, and indeed then he was not. He had definitely moved away from Marxism.

For one thing, he talked very often of "the people," the common people. This is a term used by most politicians, the American people, the British people, and it disregards the idea of classes. Marx's theory was of classes, and that only the working-class, in a highly industrialized nation, could make a Socialist revolution. Therefore Lenin and Trotsky knew that in fact for Russia it was an impossibility. Yet they felt that they should push the revolution as far as it would go. This was the reason for the November Revolution, and if they had been following James' theories, this would have ended in February with the inevitable crushing of the uprising.

Lenin, in his *Testament,* which is given elsewhere in this book, spoke of the two classes that formed the 1917 revolution in Russia, that is the peasants and the workers.

In a speech in which James explained what the Johnson/Forest ideology was, he told his audience, he and his companions believed in eliminating political parties.

Lenin's idea of highly trained cadres was thrown over. James had strongly supported this conception when he wrote *World Revolution* in 1937. Now he discarded it so he was no longer a Leninist. He wanted no political parties of any kind. "The party formula has been exhausted, it cannot work any longer," he said.

In its place he and his new group were to envisage an organisation based on councils. It is unclear how different the organizations would be from parties. It was difficult to understand the distinction. He explained that his group in 1943 published a document called *Education, Propaganda and Organisation,* which soon had wide acceptance." I find no evidence for this.

Raya Dunayevskaya believed that the system in the U.S.S.R. under Stalin was State Capitalism, an exploded concept, which she persuaded James to accept.

I wonder how much circulation was actually achieved by the pamphlets produced by the Johnson/Forest Tendency and their few colleagues. They were paying for the printing and publishing as well as supporting James, so it is reasonable to suppose the number of copies made was not large.

And how large was their following?

James is said, in his own eyes at the end of his life, to have been a faithful disciple of Marxism and of Lenin. Since during his late years, he wanted to abolish the political party, he was certainly a Leninist no longer. He also wrote that "Marxism was discredited in the world," so was no longer a Marxist.

James impressed upon his listeners, "the lessons of personal development, understanding of culture and faith in an undying potentiality of mass movements across the world." The lessons of personal development might well have come from Dale Carnegie. Understanding soap operas as culture is difficult to swallow. To believe in the undying potentiality of mass movements across the world is very fine and idealistic, but it does not define what these mass movements should be, when the potentiality of a mass movement could as easily be one of Fascism as of any social revolution.

In his review of the Hungarian Revolution in *Facing Reality*, in 1958, Paul Buhle for the first time seems critical, for he says the text approached as close as ever, to "an anarchist philosophy." In fact, a great deal of his later philosophy was anarchistic. James' insistence that it was the masses that needed to make a revolution is undoubtedly true and one that has never been denied. In fact Trotsky says, "It is the masses that makes the engine go." That is without the masses there could be no revolution. That is so fundamental, so obvious that it is difficult to see how it could have been made into an argument.

To make his Johnson/Forest group important, James said about a document published in 1941 called *Socialist Society,* 72 pages:

". . . and there for the first time we suggested that Stalinism was not a party that had gone wrong . . . Stalin was a new type of leader and a new type of intellectual leader who would take charge . . . a trade's union leader."

So Stalin becomes a trade's union type leader. It is certainly an original view but one that most people would not find valid.

He continues:

"All over the country they were reading it." (His pamphlet)

In an evaluation of another pamphlet published by the group, *State Capitalism and World Revolution,* James says:

"It stands substantially today as the best analysis you can find anywhere of the development of the Russian Revolution and the revolutionary movement."

James also says:

"Trotsky's theories and basic ideas in which he proved that 'Stalin . . . would restore capitalism in Russia,' was utterly false and wrong."

Alas, as we see today, Stalinism has led his successors to restore capitalism in Russia. For the people wanting a market economy are old Communists such as Yeltsin.

In a further speech again later back in England, James suggests that his article *The Negro Question in the United States,* "was recognized by all Communist parties, and the rest of them all, as the best analysis of the Negro question which had ever been done by a Marxist movement in the United States. It is still today the best."

In another speech, in which he was clearly trying to aggrandize his small group, to an audience that would have no means of evaluating it, he said:

"The Third International and Trotsky's (Fourth), have all fallen apart, and nobody else has any doctrine or idealogy. As I say, when you get to a certain height above the others (you see) . . . that which others on the level below do not see." So he made himself and his group Olympians.

He explains: How his non-party organization would work.

"Give classes. Publish a journal or one or two pages. These are for the organizers and not for the public. The paper should be divided into sections coordinated by the organizers. There should be articles on the undeveloped countries, on Africa, on the West Indies and on Great Britain: also on economic questions and with literary questions, including review of books."

Were workers to read all the subjects or were they to be for the edification of the non-party organizers? It is difficult to be clear how this organisation, with its journal, differed from the ones of known political parties. *FIGHT* had had articles, excellent articles, month after month, for many years, covering the many important political events of the era, from the viewpoint of The Workers' Party of the Fourth International.

James sent all his books to me except those of the Johnson/Forest period. In fact, during those years, when he was surrounded by numerous women, our contact was slight.

I had all his earlier books. He sent me the *Moby Dick* book after he returned to England in the Fifties.

Nello then sent me *Modern Politics,* when he was back in the States, with an inscription from Hofstra College in 1969. This is not really a book, but six speeches he gave in the public library in Trinidad in 1960. He says the speeches were not prepared but given extemporaneously. They are poorly printed, amount to only sixty-eight pages. On the front inside cover, there are two small advertisements. One is for Angostura Bitters and the other for Limasol, a refreshing facial liquid against heat.

I imagine that these helped pay for the printing of the collection of speeches. However, it is treated seriously as a book by his admirers. Parts of it were again reprinted in the gathering together of his speeches and articles in the three hard cover books edited by Anne Grimshaw in the eighties.

I do not know why he waited so long to send it to me. Its pages are now yellow with age, but I like it because it has a photograph of him, which must be an earlier one than taken at sixty because it looks like the Nello I knew thirty years earlier.

His cricket book, *Beyond the Boundary,* he sent via my brother. He also sent me *Amistad I,* in which he had an excellent article on the *African Slave Trade.* This was published in 1970, a year later, but I do not know when I received it.

In his book on cricket, which brought James into the limelight in

England and then in the States, he deals with cricketers, with poets, philosophers and artists, more than he does with politics or with revolutionaries. He suggests that the fielding of a ball, the hitting of a ball, a stroke, will take us to a far more fundamental consideration of life, and that the response to physical action or vivid representation of it, is necessary, because we are made that way. For unknown centuries survival for us, like all other animals depended upon competent and effective physical activity. He says further, another name for the perfect flow of motion is style, or if you will, significant form. In another place he writes, "professionalism, will produce the poetic, artistic, or philosophical qualities which will make the great athelete and the great cricketer of the future." He makes the suggestion that the case of West Indian self-government— and "it is not cricket"—"have come together:" that is, that the need for self-government and the fair-play as shown in cricket on the English playing fields.

He said "I was never very forthcoming, but the British people represented the ideal of what I was doing. That was the British I knew." So in his book on cricket, he links cricket to the English sense of fair-play.

His cricket book is partly autobiographical. He tells us a great deal about himself or rather his own image of himself.

He writes:

"When I left school (at 18), I was an educated person. . . . I became a respectable and self-respecting member of society."

This is far removed from being a Marxist, which he was not after his break with Trotskyism, but which he still claimed to be on various occasions.

He goes on to tell one of his audiences about his book on cricket as "the finest book that has ever been writen on cricket in Great Britain. That is the general opinion."

He then goes back to the earlier books and pamphlets put out by him and his United States group:

"Now that is a fantastic achievement (they have made) . . . I would not say unexcelled, but some of them are untouched and unsurpassed in the whole history of the revolutionary movement."

Again, he built up the work of that small group he formed when he broke with the Trotskyist party. He repeats his assertion:

"Now this is an astonishing series of achievements, absolutely astonishing, there is nothing in the movement that I know anywhere like it."

James writes:

"In 1940, came a crisis in my political life. I rejected the Trotskyist version of Marxism and set about to re-examine and reorganize my view of the world, which was (and remains) essentially a political one. It took more than ten years, but by 1952, I once more felt my feet on solid ground and in consequence I planned a series of books. The first was published as the most concrete point reached in the analysis of human possibilities and socialism."

James felt it was as surely a form of art equal to the opera and the ballet. One can only say that James' ideas were certainly individualistic.

Because of James' final political ideal of city-states, in particular Athens, and based on its Olympic sports and its many great names nurtured in its culture, it is necessary to look back briefly on Greek history.

Despite the fantastic developments in Athens for twenty-five years, the city-states of Greece in that period were constantly at war, and their democracy and culture were built on slavery.

Can this in any was be a political model for the 21st century? After the Darian invasion, five hundred years before the birth of Christ, the peoples of Greece under the divisive influence of geography and the great variety of tribes, developed the city-states: small settlements, which grew into minor kingdoms. However, Greece was dependent largely on agriculture, which remained poor. While not great mariners, the Greeks did have access to the sea. Through this they obtained colonies which also became city-states. The cities developed independently and separately. Elites grew into aristocracies and these produced monarchies and tyrants. There was limited democracy based on slavery. Contests such as the Olympic games fostered some unity between the city-states. But they were poorly united in the Persian Wars. However, out of this successful war, Athens grew in size and developed a civilization and culture which was to have great influence on the rest of the Western world. It was in this period that the men with the great names we know, lived and produced their works in philosophy, drama, sculpture, architecture: Aeschylus, Aristophanes, Plato, Aristotle, Euripides, Hippocrates. Yet Athens lasted little more than twenty-five years until its war with Sparta. The years were 431 to 404 B.C. Then the warring states were defeated by Philip II of Macedonia, who conquered Greece. His son, Alexander the Great, in his military victories spread the ideas of Greek culture and civilization. However, the Greek city-state became weaker and weaker through their constant warfare until they fell into the hands of the Roman Empire.

Even Paul Buhle admits:

"Certainly his (James) conception of modern politics as a civic exercise, taking up where the Greek City State left off, had little realistic relation to the troubled context of Third World national liberations."

Jean Paul Sartre writes:

"The European elite (the colonizers) picked out promising adolescents: they branded them, as with a red hot iron, with the principles of western culture. She (the Mother Country) had created a new breed, the Greco-Latin Negroes."

Was C.L.R. James one of them? He was certainly highly impressed by Greek athletes and scholars, whose standards he set for cricketers in his book *Beyond A Boundary*. He wanted no highly educated party leading the banded masses. He talks of some workers rioting against the police. Here is no standing leader whom masses follow because of his great achievements in the past. Here is no previously prearranged plan. They met, they shouted, and stormed off.

What did this move of going against the police station mean? It certainly did not mean a revolution. It was one single episode among thousands and thousands of such episodes that occur all the time, or at least hundreds and hundreds of such episodes that occur all the time. They do not amount to anything. This statement was made when he was eighty years old. And he says that though he is old and dying, he has the satisfaction of knowing that capitalism is collapsing all over the world. Again he was wrong as he had been wrong in so many times in his writings on his prophecies of the future. That he could see the assault of a few youths against a police station as a revolution shows how far he had come from any tenets of Marxism or Leninism. He also thought that out of the present barbarianism would come new states of society that would allow mankind to develop qualities and characteristics for which people have been struggling for many centuries. It was a completely unrealistic final statement of an old man. Did he not know of the children who were dying there, thousands of homeless who existed in the cities of America; that so many lacked the human basic necessities of food and shelter, health care, education? These are not the people to make a revolution; to make a revolution you have to have hope. To a great extent they become robots as in Orwell's *1984;* but James could end his life on an optimistic note for the future of mankind, for which there was no basis.

During the McCarthy era, James was so afraid of being caught up in the witch hunting net that he gave up making political speeches and instead gave public lectures on American literature. It was these, in fact, that formed the basis of his book on Herman Melville, on *Moby Dick*. James then sent copies of the book to every U.S. congressman hoping by this that someone would plead his case so that he could stay in the States. This means that he in no way wanted to be considered a revolutionary or a political figure at all. Unfortunately for him, none of the U.S. congressmen were too much impressed and James was deported.

As in the States, and in his early days in London, so he drew around him a group of admirers again in his last days. He became an "eminence grise" in his old age and he loved it.

But he had traveled a strange zigzag path to achieve it, far from the one we had traveled together in his youth.

15
James and His Late Admirers

I REPRODUCE PART OF A POEM WRITTEN IN MEMORY OF C. L. R. James:

> "O great seer & prophet of the Real
> we miss your scintillating ideas of the Present
> We miss your scholastic & Jazzy tone poems to the
> Future. We miss your spaceage theories of this very
> moment oscillating in our everyday historical memory.
> C'mon back & play with us some more!
> We need your amazing skill & ancient wisdom
> We need your brilliant logic & sci-fi insight
> We need your limitless truth & quirky understandings
> We need you out here on the edge of our liberated lives
> way out here 'beyond a boundary'"

Was this my old love? I do not find evidence of his seemingly manifold talents. Did I and do I still miss qualities and capabilities that others saw in him in his late years? Love is supposed to be blind. Am I too wide-eyed?

One admirer of James, a reviewer of Paul Buhle's book, *C.L.R. James: The Artist As Revolutionary*, writes, "We the Lilliputians he will leave behind, will simply have to step back and approach him piecemeal."

It was not until he broke away and formed the Johnson/Forest group did the admiration begin to appear. This was mostly amongst a few young women because James was sexually very attractive. But even here "Forest" made a break with him because she did not think he was treating her as an equal, as she evidently thought she was.

Amongst black men, Nkrumah was young, not yet politically seasoned, who was ready to seek advice from James. But the correspondence with him was greatly carried on by another member of the group, Grace Lee.

Have Nkrumah, Padmore, Manley, Kenyatta, Robeson, or others

among African and West Indian leaders, ever used such terms of James as Renaissance Man, Man of the Century, or Twentieth Century Giant, etc.? Have any of the great writers, thinkers, philosophers of our times ever laid such floral wreaths of praise at his feet?

James was certainly not unwilling to aggrandize his own work and value to the young academics he met. Journalists gave him good reviews, but did his age help build the acclaim he received when he was an octogenarian?

The fact that he was black would tend to give him too a glamor that a white man would not obtain at least, in England.

I see in one of the articles about him by an admirer that James was never a popular man amongst the masses. But was not that what James tried to accomplish, the creation of mass movement, first a white one and then a black one? The writer says that James was "too much of a gentleman of the old school. Racial rhetoric is beneath him."

Are we then to disdain the rhetoric of Martin Luther King, Jr., or of Jessie James against the injustices against their race in the United States? Are we to adopt gentlemanly poses when we talk or write of the masses' wrongs?

Then why, when he was young, did he strongly, and so well, call to a great crowd in Trafalgar Square to stand against World War II?

I have read and re-read every book he wrote, every article, every transcription of his speeches. I have tried scrupulously to follow every step he took, every endeavor in which he embarked, every activity of his over the years.

I find I cannot stand with his modern admirers.

I find him often a pervertor of the truth in such instances of which I know. There are the many contradictions of his political stands. There are many wrong analyses to be found in his writings. There are so many of his statements that can be found to be false.

Do I wish to topple the idol? Show the feet are of clay?

I remember him fondly, and I want to continue to remember him fondly. I never knew and do not recognize this inflated figure that is now offered me.

Buhle writes:

"Generations of Western radicals have gone to school with the ideas of James, Gandhi . . . "

This equating James with Gandhi just does not make sense.

Gandhi's name and ideas are known to the millions and millions of people that make up that great country of India. Every literate person in the whole world knows the name of Gandi and knows of his ideas.

Not everyone, even in his own small island of Trinidad, knows the name of James. He gave speeches for a year in East and West Africa but it is doubtful if more than a few know his name and work.

In the United States his name is not well-known except by a few at the universities. Blacks in Federal City University and Howard University who heard him lecture may well remember him, and some of their successors may read his books.

Most North American blacks know the names of DuBois, Marcus Garvey, Stokely Carmichael, James Baldwin, The Black Panthers, Le Roi Jones, Rap Brown, Martin Luther King, Jr., Malcom X, Paul Robeson, Fidel Castro, Lumumba. They too have heard of Gandhi, but not of C.L.R. James. Even in the 1970 revolts in Trinidad, his native land, James's name was not on the banners.

Everyone acknowledges that James's finest work was *The Black Jacobins*. When he was writing that was when I knew him. I wish he had written ten such works.

A serious study of the man, his talents and his faults, of his work, some of it excellent and some of it failures, would do more honor to him, than the outpouring of adulation that he has been accorded.

Let me select for illustration, the praises poured out on to him by two of his admirers, Paul Buhle, his biographer, and Margaret Busby, who wrote an Introduction to a selection of his writings.

Buhle writes: "It was likely, the first time since leaving Moscow that Trotsky had met with a self-confident political equal."

In exile, Trotsky had received many intellectual sympathizers. Did they view James as an equal? No.

Equating James with Trotsky is far and away a too high level of adulation. For this was a meeting in 1939, at a time I still knew James, having seen him in 1938 and again in 1940.

I had always considered myself James's intellectual equal in the years of our companionship. If I had gone to work for Trotsky, I would have gone as a disciple. Trotsky is a world renowned figure. James is known only to a few.

In 1933, almost at the same time that C. L. R. formed our London group, Trotskyist groups were being formed in South Africa, after the earlier crushing of the black movement there, in the 1920's. As in England, they were mainly bourgeoisie, but black bourgeoisie. This means, however, that Trotsky had an interest in all black movements, not only in those of the United States. Here was a Russian, a white man, an exile, having influence in Africa before James gave politics his attention.

Nello had sent me after it was published, his small book on *Modern Politics*. I found myself in disagreement with most of his theses. These were not the ones that he espoused when I knew him.

In the books I have read about him recently, which quote conversations he had with various people, there were often quite untrue statements or perversions of the truth. For instance, he is quoted as saying about United States and British Trotskyists, amongst which he founded our group, "I left them. That is answer enough." He did not leave us except to go to the States, and his deprecation of us is unworthy of him, since we were his loyal group, young and idealistic and hard working, for what was then his cause. The United States group had been generous to him too. He had not been generous to them.

He was certainly beginning to have some ideological differences with Trotsky's views, but he left us only because he had been invited to visit the States by the Socialist Workers' Party of the U.S.A., who paid his expenses to get there and to support him. He made no break with the Trotskyists before he left London; even though he was beginning to have some reservations. He was still attending meetings of the group in 1938.

Alas, in the Thirties, the James I knew and loved was not the man who was eulogized in the Eighties, when he was drawing around himself a crowd of young admirers, who depended a great deal on his own estimation of himself.

In every sphere, he magnified his role.

According to the Minutes of a meeting on August 10, 1936, when at least two Trotskyist groups joined together, it was agreed that L. Cripps, Marsillier and James (voted in that order), were to make up the editorial committee of *FIGHT*, B. Matlow, an M.P. was to be managing editor and May Matlow was to be editorial secretary. James was not at the meeting, therefore he was not the founder of *FIGHT* and was only co-editor with myself and Marsillier. Both of his admirers, however, give him the titles of founder and editor.

Some of James's articles were included in *FIGHT*, as well as some of mine and of other members of the two groups. No articles were signed, so it is difficult to tell at this stage who wrote which articles. On the frontispiece of the paper, there was no mention of the name of an editor. Either his admirers made him *the* Editor, or he told them it was so. It is a small point but one that shows how his work has been aggrandized in this and other spheres. The paper continued to appear after James left for the States.

The only author's name ever given in *FIGHT* was that of Trotsky, when we reproduced some part of his writings about current events. These we were proud to include after having received his consent.

Margaret Bushy is also over-admiring because James knew Latin and Greek. Trinidad's schools were modeled on British schools. Every middle-class school boy, so there would be thousands and thousands of them at the time, would all have been taught Greek and Latin. So it was not special. School girls learned Latin, and knew Greek literature only in English. All had to pass matriculation for university by an examination in Latin.

Again, a great point is made of the fact that James, a teacher, put on a Shakespearean play (I am intrigued that it was *Othello*). In England at all schools, plays of Shakespeare were produced each year, at least in his time and my time. It was therefore not special or innovative of James, for I imagine colonial schools followed this pattern.

Margaret Busby is also impressed that James was reading Thackeray at eight years old. So was I and my contemporaries. I have checked with other English friends and all say with me that they never remembered learning to read. All of us read the classics early. Dickens was my favorite author, but I also read Thackeray.

Buhle says that C. L. R. will look different, more complete, more understandable from the mid-twenty-first century than from today's perspective. He therefore suggests that none of us are sufficiently intellectual to understand fully what a great man James was. He goes on to say that he has been the "Renaissance Man" and Black Plato.

James describes himself in his cricket book as "a Puritan," and talks of his "Puritan soul," and that he had early learnt the English Public School Code. He describes his family, including himself, "always present as the Puritan, the sense of discipline."

Did he really see himself as a Puritan? If so, it would seem a charming innocence or, at the time it was written in the Sixties, a desire to be known as "respectable." For his life was scarcely one of a Puritan. At one period, he was drinking heavily in his life when matters were not going well for him. But there was always the subject of money. James was supported for most of his adult life by other people. No Puritan would condone such conduct. They would regard it as a lack of self-respect, a lack of self-reliance. They would certainly disapprove of his relationships with many women.

Looking back and reviewing his history, his politics and his writing, I also reflect on his relationships with other women. Probably the adjustments of marriage were too difficult for him say many late admirers. He was a Third World novelist, a keen sports critic, a leading historian, an African theorist and spokesman, great pioneer of importance and a great philosopher of universal scope.

Gerald Guiness, an English professor at the University of Puerto Rico, writing an "In Memoriam" article about Gordon Lewis, says of him:

"Surely no one in Puerto Rico—perhaps even in English-speaking Caribbean—wrote better English. Here was writing that was always lucid, acerbic, warmhearted and witty . . . "

"Like Trinidadian historian C. L. R. James, Lewis may ultimately be remembered as much for his contribution to Caribbean literature as for his academic work in history and social thought. If so, he would join the ranks of Macauley, Gibbon and Carlyle, all masters of *English* prose."

It is interesting that the two men, both good friends of mine, should be so linked together. Gordon Lewis was a better prose writer than James. Gordon Lewis had the better mind, and the better educational background.

Nello called himself "an educated man." Gordon would never have thought of doing so. Nello would say on more than one occasion that he did not like Gordon. Gordon never retaliated.

But it is interesting that admirer Guiness calls C. L. R. a historian. Except for *The Black Jacobins,* James wrote no other history. Perhaps one book, if sufficiently good, is enough for fame.

To refute these many claims would need a whole book so that it is only possible for me to answer a few of them. First of all, he wrote, except for some very early stories, only one novel, *Minty Alley*. As I read and corrected the galleys for that book, I felt that it was very much a first novel and I was indeed quite surprised that he had been able to have it published. People have claimed it his description of a black working-class; the people of *Minty Alley* are definitely not proletariats. They are "lumpen," their characteristics generally ugly.

His being a West Indian and Third World novelist, with just one early novel, is hardly true. He was a keen sports critic, of course. A leading historian, admirers say. He wrote very little history: his most famous and memorable book, one that will be important, was *The Black Jacobins,* the story of the Haitian revolt in the early 19th century, the black masses against both the local white population and Napoleon. This is outstanding work. I myself helped with that by going and checking with sources in the British Museum, and I also went over the manuscript with him. To call him an African theorist and spokesman, claims are greatly exaggerated. That he was a faithful disciple of Marx and Lenin, is definitely not true. He was that when he was in the Trotsky movement; when he moved away from it this definitely does not stand as a statement of his principles. In regard to Lenin, one of Lenin's most important contributions was the need for a party of highly trained cadres to lead the revolutionary movement. James later wanted only a spontaneous rising of people without any leadership.

I myself wrote a history of Russia which took me four-and-a-half years and my Harvard-educated, Russian-born husband looked into the Russian sources for me. There were numerable rebellions against the Czarist regime in the various centuries. Some of them had leaders throughout that time. People were rebelling against their conditions but had no leadership that fully understood what had to be done until Lenin. Almost all spontaneous uprisings in history have been crushed.

Another point made by his admirers is that at one time James was selected by his party to debate publicly with Bertrand Russell. Buhle says by the vote of the audience, James won. However, this in no way puts him on the intellectual level of Bertrand Russell.

Bertrand Russell told me that he was always petrified of public speaking, that he was immobilized and found it difficult to mount the steps to the platform. When there, his mind went blank and he was sure he would be speechless before the microphone. Naturally a young black orator would win against him.

When "Bertie" was making a joke there was a movement in his long neck and the sound of his chuckle, somewhat like a turkey's gobble. The jokes were small sophisticated ones enjoyed mostly by himself. Few popular audiences saw the sophisticated point of them. Certainly James would be the victor in a speaking contest against him.

Interestingly, Buhle writes that James had "no real compulsion to reach directly the popular audience." This would seem to mean he was not a man who could or even wanted to reach the masses. He was content with his admiring coteries. I was part of his first one.

Buhle goes on to say that James insisted that only artists and international figures who truly encompassed diverse worlds within themselves can cast a shadow into the future, and that James himself was both of these.

Buhle goes further, saying that James's long intellectual life from childhood window-gazing at Trinidadian cricket and his onward relentless geriatic television watching, that is in his old age his constant watching of soap operas, he has used the available vehicles of mass consciousness including his own, to apprehend the untested capacities of ordinary people. That therein lies a singular strength.

The word again used is ordinary people. It does not deal with classes. And by a boy looking at cricket matches and an old man looking at soap operas, he can test the capabilities of ordinary people is an odd idea. I could almost go sentence by sentence through the book, but again Buhle says that James's work has yet to be taken as a whole in the sense of the equivalent of Lucas, Sutra, Gramsei or, for that matters, Lenin; and it is this juxtaposition of famous names with that of James that is used to make him such a prodigy. Buhle remarks that at an early meeting with James, he asked him why the group that he formed when he left the Trotskyist party in the States had so little influence, and James replied, "people all over the world ask about my group." Buhle says James made that statement with Leninist determination. Now, James may have made the statement determinately, but it has no relevence to Lenin at all. In fact if one wishes to think clearly about how Lenin would have replied, Lenin always answered clearly and truthfully without ambiguity, And certainly without self-aggrandizement. So in these various ways, I think Buhle particularly, by putting James beside the names of world-known figures, is the way this prodigy has been made of James: this superman in all fields of intellectual and artistic endeavors.

James wanted to be, and probably felt he was, a world figure. If that belief is strong in a man or woman, they can often get others to believe it too. It was self-delusion in which others, to his pleasure, were to give evidence. His 80th birthday speeches are meandering. His love for soap operas is incredible for an intellectual. In one of his speeches years later, about the Johnson/Forest group, James said: "In 1943, we published a document called *Education, Propaganda and Organization*. It is still there to be read. Nobody bothered with it at the start but after two years . . . all the world asked about us."

I can only put in a big question mark here.

The pamphlet was only mimeographed when it was issued by his United States group in 1943, though later it was re-issued as Facing Reality, in 1968 by his admirers, twenty-five years later, when a search was on for every piece of his own, or his writings with others, or the text of any speech by him that could be found in his fifty years of political activity and lectures.

In the end, he and they were aggrandizing every word he spoke, every word he wrote.

Having such ardent admirers at his bedside in his last years must have been very satisfying for James' vanity.

He must have died in a happy state. But the assessment of his talents and influence by his admirers is overwrought. I think his influence, in the many fields that both Paul Buhle and Margaret Busby mention, has been small. The evidence is apparent in an unbiased examination of his work.

Busby, writing the introduction to the collection of James' articles, pamphlets, and speeches in 1984, in *C.L.R. James At The Rendezvous Of Victory,* makes his early work become the emergence of an indigenous West Indian literature. *The Life of Captain Cipriani* becomes a pioneer work arguing the case for West Indian government. There were just three chapters that dealt with the subject and James told me he had not seriously been considering this when he wrote the book.

She makes his time in the Independent Labour Party very important, and him Chairman of its Finchley branch. In our small group of a dozen or so people, I hardly think we thought of him as Chairman. It sounds like Mao-Tse-Tung.

It was under his auspices . . . "that Nkrumah . . . was to begin his preparations for the revolution which was to initiate a new Africa."

James met Nkrumah when he was in the States. He sent him with a letter to George Padmore asking help for him. In 1947, when Nkrumah left London to go to the Gold Coast, James was busy with his Johnson/Forest group, far removed from any African connection. But he did go at Nkrumah's invitation to his inaugural in Ghana and stayed on as his guest to give some speeches over a year's period. This one, short letter sent to Padmore introducing Nkrumah, hardly seems to make James into "the initiator of African independence." He did make a lecture tour in both East and West Africa in 1967–68, but some of the leaders were already established there, since they invited him to speak.

The author writes of "the struggle for colonial emancipation, in which James had continuously been involved, was by now showing some results." James is made in this build-up into an instigator of freedom in both Africa and the West Indies.

He was fifty-seven when he returned to Trinidad. Up to that time he had been active in the struggle against Stalinism, then Trotskyism, and then in his interest in fundamental Marxism. He undoubtedly still went out and gave lectures on political matters from his own newly evolved political point of view to various audiences. Obviously he no longer was considered a revolutionary threat to the Establishment. This was a very different situation from when he had been a young man. If he had been in England when the war broke out he would have undoubtedly been imprisoned. In the States, he was deported and kept interned on Ellis Island. That fiery young man however, had, it would seem, lost most of his fervor as he grew older.

When he was sent to Ellis Island for deportation, James appealed to Sir Anthony Eden to stop his deportation from the States. Amusedly, Sir Anthony replied that banishment to the United Kingdom could in no way be considered a punishment. Always C. L. R. had praise for the British. I could not understand his wanting to be an American. Was it the greater worship he received in the United States? Especially by women?

I wonder how his wives fared in that black and white situation in the United States. In many states it remained a crime for black and white persons to live together or to marry. There was one Declaration of Independence Day, where a group who had invited the mayor of Oakridge, Tennessee, to join, went on a lynching expedition of Negroes because one local black man was living in "sin" with a white woman.

I now fondly picture Nello sitting up in bed, books around him, and watching soap operas, as an old man.

It is interesting that his late admirers introduce part of a letter which James wrote to friends in New York after he had been deported to England. "It is most remarkable, but at the present moment the feeling that I have and the memory of the life in the United States are expressed most concretely in gramaphone records, jazz records in particular, and movies." That is hardly a political statement. "The founders of America guaranteed the citizens of their new democracy the right to life, liberty and the pursuit of happiness, these goals were then little more then abstract ideas in Europe. But it was from Europe, from France, from the great writers of the Enlightenment that these ideas came, and out of which in 1789 the French Revolution occurred. The new North American democracy was limited to a very few of the citizens. Votes were given not to the general public but to a small number of people, as landowners and people of a fairly high level of income.

Almost all of James's late admirers give him a particularly high place in the black movement. In the United States it was small. In Africa, it was small. It was so even in the area of his birthplace.

Two other people, admirers of James, provided an Introduction to the compilation of some of his writings on *American Civilization*, These are Anna Grimshaw and Keith Hart.

They start their Preface with: "C. L. R. James deserves to be recognized as one of the greatest writers and activists in the Marxist tradition."

I find even this first sentence difficult to accept since once James left the Troskyist fold, he ceased to be a Marxist, in fact, as I have pointed out elsewhere, he says that Marxism was finished. This meant he was a Marxist only during the time when he was in our group in London, and even as he began to move away from it as he went to the States, he soon ended being a Trotskyist. He did, at the same time, end being a Marxist. This is shown by his own repudiation of Marx on occasion after occasion.

The second sentence say his vision of the movement of world civilization encompassed his own experience of the Caribbean, where he was born, Europe, America and Africa. While he certainly knew Trinidad, that is not to say that he knew a great deal about the rest of the Caribbean despite his splendid book on Haiti. He never went there. And of Europe, he knew really only England, and to a very small degree, Paris.

He did not, as far as I know, ever go to the other countries such as Germany, Holland, Belgium, Italy, even Greece that he wrote about in the end, nor Turkey, nor the Soviet Union. This is an enormous area of Europe which he did not know. Then, America means: South America, Central America, the United States and Canada. He did not know three of those countries and knew only to some extent, the United States and also Canada.

His contribution in the colonial struggle had been small until that time. His three returns to Trinidad lasted little more than five years in all, and his belated efforts were unsuccessful. He went back when Dr. Williams was already in power.

By running a sentence together about his being "Professor of Humanities at Federal City University, Washington D.C., at Harvard, Yale, Princeton. . . ." a reader presumes James was a professor at these last three prestigious universities. He was only asked by a group of students at these last three universities to give a lecture there.

He did not act in his play "Toussaint L'Ouverture." I was there and know this was not so. His book, *World Revolution,* Margaret Busby calls an extensive history of the Third International. The "extensive" history was written within a year (James at one point says three months), with great assistance from Harry Wicks, an old ex-Communist, and much help with clippings and finding sources from our whole group. There are many wrong prophecies made in the book.

"C. L. R. James is not just a Caribbean thinker. He is a world historical figure, and certainly takes the pre-eminent place amongst 20th century thinkers." By the time he was an old man, there were a great many such tributes to him.

"C. L. R. James was one of the most remarkable writers of our generation. He is a scholar and historian, a practical politician, a cricketer with his integrating these activities into a unified life."

James had not of course achieved this great adulation when he was young or in middle life, not until the end and after his death.

He hardly took part in the U.S. in the antiwar movement, but in a speech he said: "I was treated like a dog before I went, I was treated like a dog while I was there, I was treated like a dog when I returned."

Now, the use of "I" is rather strange because people reading it would, not knowing the circumstances of James, have thought that he meant he himself, he did not use the term "we" meaning "we, the black masses." He had tried to join up, he said, in the First World War, but in 1918 when it ended, he was only seventeen. Therefore, he had taken no part whatsoever in that war. This expression, "the experiences that I received," were at least misleading as to his own role. He again was making optimistic prophesies about the future. He wrote, "I live with a presently daily expectation of the beginning of an upheaval . . . marking the beginning of the social revolution. I think of it many hours every day, it keeps me alive." This was written in 1943 when he was the leader with Raya Dunayevaskaya in the Johnson/Forest group, and so still had Marxist views.

Buhle makes him a "Pan African theorist, and spokesman of great pioneer importance." A very debatable estimation. Finally Buhle writes of him as "a philosopher of universal scope."

James' only philosophical writings were included in his cricket book, *Beyond A Boundary,* in which I find his philosophy does not compare in depth with the classical established philosophers. Philosophers tend to expand and develop their theories with age. James was not even consistent.

Buhle tries to explain James' political position. "One of the less understood facets of Jamesian politics" Buhle writes, "has been the insistance upon the obsolence of the national state."

The Soviet Union today is breaking up into national states and has already broken up its union. In Yugoslavia, there is a break-up with violent fighting between Croatian and Serbian forces.

Nationalism seems on the rise, not obsolescent.

James is said to have believed, "Perestroika is the merest preparation (that) would restore the promise of the 1917 revolution." The old Soviet Union has broken up into national states, and socialism is being superseded by a market economy.

In the conclusion of his biography of C. L. R., Buhle writes: "A

Jamesian politics for the end of the Twentieth century and beginning of a new millennium, would surely begin with wholesale changes wrought in world politics and the world economy since James effected his fullest theoretical 'system' roughly forty years ago. The breaking point appeared with the calamity of World War II and the impossibility of recovery, short of socialism."

It is now fifty years ago since James declaimed the impossibility of world recovery, short of socialism. Instead, all over the world there has been a defeat of socialism.

It is stated that James established a Black Marxism. There is no color to Marxism. Later, he foreswore Marxism.

He is also said to have "played a part in the growth of the Trotskyist movement in France." Trotsky himself was in France at the time, and his son Lev Sedov in Paris. When in Paris with me, James was not even fluent in speaking French. I doubt they needed a West Indian to help them with the party there.

He is made almost the key figure in the decolonization in Africa, in the independence in Trinidad. He did not go back until Dr. Williams was in office, and independence occurred after James had left.

He was actor, writer, speaker, philosopher, professor. "He presented the ideas, worked through in the Forties in the light of the Hungarian revolution, and the growth of rank and file shop stewards'-type movements in Europe and North America.

I did not know this super-prodigy.

Small actions are made into great ones and have small foundations. The Forties were the years of the Johnson/Forest group when he was more or less in isolation.

James wanted to be a great man, and the retinue around him at the end, gave him the assurance that he was. In a way it was part of his charm. His arrogance was in a way endearing. He had to believe he was a fine, special person. So he ended his life on that happy note.

Finally looking back at the figure at a crossroad, is a figure that would grow smaller as decades went by, but was always still there at the turn of a path however small and faint in outline it might become.

I have had several black men friends since that time. Some of them were handsome, at least one had the same bodily grace as James. Some were intelligent, respected in their various fields, a novelist, a musician. Others were working men including a Vietnam war veteran. Either they were born in the United States or came from different islands of the Caribbean or from Africa itself. One or two have been sturdier of figure. Two who came from the islands have that enchanting lilting voice nurtured from those special places in the sun, two or three have been more humdrum, who have managed a place for themselves in the white establishment.

Their eyes are dark-brown to black, bright or consciously dulled. Do they overlay that figure of the past? I wonder if any of them sense I was once a black man's love?

There has always been a good understanding, a rapport between us. They know I stand firmly on their side in the civil rights movement. But in no case have these later friendships been other than everyday.

Since neither of us, James nor I, were religious, we had no sense of sin or wrong doing. Since neither of us were conventional we had no thought of what people might say. The members of our group in no way found our love strange or unacceptable.

Except for that first moment when I was walking up the stairs of his rooming house and felt his eyes on my legs, had I a moment of hesitation. In later years, I have these other friends.

One is the well-known musician, Mmadu Onyeviva, who sings songs in eleven different languages, is guitarist and pianist, and who serenades me on each of my birthdays with calypso. The other is the author Piri Thomas.

In his most recent book, *Stories From El Barrio* published by Alfred Knopf, Inc., Piri Thomas writes in the copy he sent me.

"I am proud to be your 'hermano', for you are one of those who see justice in all its colors and believe, as we all do, in the right of self-determination for all countries, large or small, which includes our island national Puerto Rico, Boriquen, isla de encanto."

When James went back the last time to England and was established there again, he had this new coterie, but somehow by then, I believe he had been de-fanged as it were. And while he was an excellent writer with a fine mind, a brilliant orator, and did take part in working-class disputes, my feeling is that he had become no longer a dangerous person to the country, no longer the revolutionary that I knew.

It seems to me that James in his old age had become acceptable to the Establishment. He had written his book on cricket in 1963. This was republished in 1983. It was given excellent reviews by all the Establishment press including the *London Times*. It was given wide acclaim. He was found generally acceptable then.

James was asked to give a series of talks on Shakespeare on the BBC. One of the plays that he talked about was *Othello;* I wonder as he talked about it, if he thought back to a time when we had seen Robeson play that role, when we were in the audience together and that had touched off and sparked our love affair. I feel that he surely then must have remembered me as *his* Desdemona. So long ago. So very long ago.